Praise for Diamonds in the Rough

"Coach Puryear is uniquely qualified to write this book. His story and the story of East Lake reflect what is good, bad, and most importantly what is possible in our lives if we will follow his lead and embody a service mind and heart."

— Tyrone Willingham, Head Football Coach at Stanford University, University of Notre Dame and University of Washington

"A heroic tale of one black man shining his light on those often assumed as less fortunate, but are they?"

— Jermel Nakia, actor (NBC's This Is Us)

"Sam Puryear's new book depicts the life he has traveled with his faith and calling for serving youth. This is a must read for everyone; golfers and non-golfers alike. It will touch your heart."

— Ed Mitchell, Ed Mitchell Technologies

"Sam did an outstanding job securing PGA Tour support for [the film From the Rough]. He continues to be a highly valued advisor to me."

— Mike Critelli, retired CEO from Pitney Bowles, entrepreneur, health care consultant, feature film producer, speaker

Diamonds
in the
ROUGH

The Shining Success Story of Inspiration,
Faith and Hope in East Lake

Diamonds
in the
ROUGH

Samuel G. Puryear, Jr.

Pure Swing Publishing

Published by Pure Swing Publishing

ISBN: 978-1-7345790-4-8

Edited by David Aretha
Cover and interior design by Christy Collins, Constellation Book Services

Some names have been changed to protect the privacy of individuals. In order to maintain their anonymity, the author may have changed some identifying characteristics and details such as physical properties, occupations and places of residence.

Printed in the United States of America

DEDICATION

This book is dedicated to my parents, Samuel G. Puryear, Sr. and Barbara W. Puryear. They gave me the guidance, belief and support which enabled me to realize that anything is possible. God allows our dreams to come true.

CONTENTS

ACKNOWLEDGMENTS

"Let them give thanks to the Lord for his unfailing love
and his wonderful deeds for mankind, for he satisfies
the thirsty and fills the hungry with good things."

(Psalm 107:8-9)

There are so many wonderful people that I would love to acknowledge because they enabled me to try to be the best version of myself. Before I thank anyone on the outside of the Puryear household, I have to thank those who resided inside. I definitely have to thank my family.

I am very appreciative of my three children. Tony, Brooke, and Cameron were absolutely amazing during this unscripted journey through East Lake. They sacrificed me, their lives, and our time. They shared their vacations with the East Lake family. They ate a plethora of meals without me. They served as my backbone in allowing me to chase my dreams. I also realized I missed a lot of little league basketball games, and I unfortunately was tardy to different events during a lot of developmental years.

Brooke and I did have a great run while I served as her little league basketball coach in Lilburn, Georgia. We went undefeated for two consecutive years and Brooke learned a lot. It manifested when she played and started on her high school basketball team. It was fun watching Cameron play soccer through snow flurries living in Michigan and watching her play hoops in middle school in Charlotte. It was incredible to fly in and watch Tony play four years of college football at

Johnson C. Smith University in Charlotte. I tried to find a balance. I felt as if God held my hand. He ordered my steps. My family and I still have conversations about the good ole days. The kids are always excited to see them. My son and several of the boys are in regular contact.

My youngest daughter, Cameron, always looked up to the East Lake boys as big brothers. In her mind, she had more big brothers than any of her friends. I would also like to thank my parents, Samuel G. Puryear Sr. and Barbara W. Puryear. Many of the disciplines that I carried to Atlanta were derived from what I learned at home. I never needed a television role model. My two role models resided in my house. They instilled in me that my actions spoke volumes but my mouth only uttered words. I was also taught that it is always better to give than receive.

I would definitely like to thank my brother Eric. He has had an incredible personal and professional career. He has coached football at several high schools and universities. He is also a wonderful father. I have leaned on him for advice and transparency when I've needed it. I actually give him the credit for me becoming a collegiate golf coach. During one of our regular conversations, he referenced the golf coach at his university. He laughed and said, "Man, you should get into college coaching. He said you deal with bigger budgets, know the game better, and you can relate to diverse groups of kids." He said, "You would win on this level." I guess he knew what he was talking about or at least that's what my six championship rings signify.

I definitely have to thank several coaches and true experts in their chosen field. These people gave me their most valuable resource, which is time. I listened, learned, and adapted. I must start by thanking my collegiate coach Dr. Catana Starks. Coach Starks gave me the framework and a working blueprint of what successful collegiate golf coaches look like. I have to thank Stanford University Head Coach Conrad Ray for giving me an opportunity. He realized that I was a nontraditional selection, but he had the courage to hire a guy who could really help his program at Stanford. I had come out of the junior golf ranks and I was an African American. There aren't many guys like Conrad in the collegiate ranks. I also have to thank Hall of Fame NFL Coach Bill Walsh. He allowed me an opportunity to pick his brain. I definitely have to thank NFL and NCAA Coach Tyrone Willingham. Coach Willingham has been an amazing mentor. He is the true definition of selfless. He is always honest and transparent with me. He doesn't tell me what he thinks I want to hear. He makes himself available and he has answered my calls and given his time trying to help me navigate the complex world of collegiate athletics and life. I definitely have to thank my golfing mentor Ed Mitchell and Ed Mitchell Technologies. He has helped increase my golf IQ in the world of golf equipment and performance. These beautiful people also allowed me to slide in a deluge of personal questions. I am always trying to create a better version of myself. I will forever be grateful for their time and assistance.

I would also like to thank a bunch of the volunteers and friends that played an integral role in my success. Pastor Fred Hartley, Rocky Rief, Mrs. Janet and Mr. Willie, Laura Tyson Puryear, Kim Woulard, Melissa Delaquis, Bobby Daugherty, Mike Perpich, Jeff Taylor, Mike Myers, my TSU contingent, Chris "Freak" Hayes and family, "Drewski Love" Morton, Gladys Torres, Snowbird and Tracy and the kids, volunteers during Tour Championship week, Sedrick Jackson, Evelyn Thompson, Tosha Arriola, Tony Smith, Sharon Thomas, Andrew Afflick, Nyre Williams, Sheldon Holloway, Jeff Dunovant, Teresa and Tatia Ross, the East Lake Board, the East Lake Junior Golf Academy Board, Dr. Carter at Southside, R. C. Pruit, the entire YMCA family, the entire East Lake Foundation family (old and new), East Lake Golf Club, Mr. Cousins, Charlie Harrison, Tom Wamsley, LPGA players Kim Williams and Stephanie Louden, the American Junior Golf Family, Drew Riefenberger, Phil Sharpe, Chris Millard, my friends in Louisville, Beth Espy, Kestrel Communication, Bobby Reardon (deceased), Ned Simon, Guy Harris, Leon Gilmore, Scarlett Pressley-Brown, John Anthony (deceased), April Lloyd, Chris Tucker, Norris Tucker, Tammy Tucker, Ray Grant and his family, Byron Williams, Cindy Chenier, Sid Corum, Lee and Sharon Elder, Shawn Huff and his family, Lew Horne, the brothers of Alpha Phi Alpha, Robert Muhammad and family, the folks in Ebony Hills, Marcus Polk, Terry Powers, the local Atlanta golf community, the

PGA Superstore family, Ted Pio Roda, Redo, Regina, Dave Shaw, Cathy Hampton and the folks at U.S. Franchise Systems, Sharon Thomas, George at the Barber Shop, Hustleman, and your boy Big Block.

There are so many people who did something to help me succeed in my job. I am indebted to everyone who helped the kids with their schoolwork, people who were willing to talk with them about life, people who took them to golf tournaments, people who took any amount of their personal time to make a difference. I am sure I have probably forgotten a few people. Please forgive me if you were left off the list, but you are not left out of my heart. I am indeed beholden. It is because of you that all of this was possible.

FOREWORD

Golf is an amazing game. It has been my life's work and it is still giving me things today after a 40-year love affair. The game tests every possible thing about a person, including his or her physical capabilities, instincts, emotions, perception, tenacity, grit, honesty, love, and relationships. It is a game that brings people together, but has also kept people apart. It is a game where people make millions of dollars and are on TV every day, while others struggle to make a livable wage. The hard work is never seen and definitely means more. Golf provides a backdrop for social conversation, as well as heated debate. People play golf to escape and also to become more present. There are doglegs on every course just like in everyday life. The game is special.

Diamonds in the Rough was written by Sam Puryear, who is also special. Sam was the very first assistant coach I hired at Stanford Men's Golf 15 years ago. He was also the first full-time assistant golf coach that our storied program had ever had. To my knowledge, Sam was also the first African American coach at the top levels of Division I collegiate golf, let alone the first to be a part of an NCAA championship team as a coach. We accomplished this feat in 2007. Sam isn't afraid to break down walls and build people up. His life experiences before Stanford University shaped who he is, and his role in the lives of the young people who were part of the East Lake Junior Golf Academy were formed with compassion and love.

The story of the young men in this book is an amazing firsthand narrative of how the game of golf helped shaped the lives of people in a positive way. The game of golf has proven that anything is possible. This story highlights the perseverance of young people overcoming some incredible odds. The East Lake Junior Golf Academy allowed these young people to reshape their futures and create new expectations for their lives. Mr. Tom Cousins helped provide resources that were utilized to accomplish things that no one would have ever bet possible, and the entire East Lake community was crowned the winner.

Sam Puryear was there for it all and he was part of the transformation. Sam's first days at the academy, the people he touched, his connections with the locals, his relationship with Mr. Cousins, his own personal upbringing, his coaching philosophy, his thoughtful mentors, and the community he was able to build are all brought to light in this fascinating story that will leave you in admiration of what positive thinking, a don't-give-up attitude, and love for the greatest game in the world can do. Who knows, maybe there are diamonds that you can discover while in the rough… instead of your golf ball!

I hope you enjoy this book as much as I did.

Conrad Ray

Conrad Ray, the Knowles Family Director of Men's Golf at Stanford University, has led his team to four Pac-12 championships, 13 NCAA Men's Golf Championships appearances, and two NCAA national championships (2007, 2019). He is a two-time NCAA Division I Coach of the Year and four-time Pac-12 Coach of the Year. In 2011, he was inducted into the NCGA Hall of Fame and in 2017, he was inducted into the Golf Coaches Association of America Hall of Fame.

PREFACE

In 1977, I was told that if my desire was to be a collegiate or professional football coach, I should learn the game of golf. I thought at the time that was a strange connection of football employment and professional success. But the game would serve to introduce people into my life with shared values. By playing a round of golf it would provide the opportunity to know these people on a much deeper level than from a simple handshake and hello. Golf offered the opportunity in a few hours to get acquainted with the real person. Therefore, I consider golf a tripwire for the discovery of their integrity, personality, and mental toughness.

In 2007, I met Sam Puryear, the first African American assistant golf coach in the PAC-10 (now PAC-12). Consequently, I was the first African American head coach to win the PAC-10 football championship and take a team to the Rose Bowl Game, in 2000. But Sam's accomplishment surpassed mine when he and head coach Conrad Ray led the Stanford Cardinal to the 2007 NCAA national championship. As coaches we both shared not only our firsts as African American successes, but also our love of golf and our love of service to others.

It was written by Corrie Ten Boom that "The measure of a life, after all, is not its duration but its donation."

I label this donation as "service." I believe that my life as a coach and everyone's life, private or professional, should be about service. This service should manifest itself in a multitude of forms in our lives. A husband serves his wife, serves his children, serves his job, serves his employees, serves his country and his God. It is through our acts of service that we show our love and respect for self and humanity.

This is where Coach Puryear is uniquely qualified to write this contribution to the enrichment of our lives. As referenced in these pages he has seen and worked with lives in their many forms: the good, the bad, the indifferent. His story and the story of East Lake reflect what is good, bad, and most importantly what is possible in our lives if we will follow his lead and embody a service mind and heart.

Tyrone Willingham
Head Football Coach, Stanford University, 1995-2001
Head Football Coach, University of Norte Dame, 2002-2004
Head Football Coach, University of Washington, 2005-2008

CHAPTER 1

Arrested on the 18th Green

"'No weapon formed against you shall prosper, and every tongue which rises against you in judgement you shall condemn. This is the heritage of the servants of the Lord, and their righteousness is from me,' says the Lord."
(Isaiah 54:17)

As Southside High School seniors Willie Brown, Shelton Davis, Brandon Bradley, and Rod Lowery stand on the 18th tee gazing down at the green, one thing becomes simplistically obvious. This is the final hole of a crazy round of golf. It is a typical Atlanta hot day. The golf shirts that the guys are wearing are sweated through from front to back. They could care less. They simply love golf and people.

All four boys are the antithesis of antisocial. They have travelled abroad and they seem to know everyone who enters the clubhouse doors. They are also creative enough to understand that every round they play against each other better be played as if it's their "major" championship. Bragging rights in the neighborhood means a lot more than the coveted "green jacket." If I were being truthful based on their lifestyle, they wouldn't know what to do with it or have anywhere to wear the jacket anyway. But being from Atlanta, this is their Masters Tournament and the 18th hole here at the Charlie Yates Golf Course is their Amen Corner, in more ways than one.

In the late 1990s, the East Lake Community Foundation and Cousins Properties partnered with Rees Jones, the renowned golf course architect, to construct the Charlie Yates Golf Course as a nice playable alternative to the famed East Lake Golf Club. The course was literally located across the street from ELGC in East Atlanta. The northwest corner of the club is where Atlanta and Decatur meet, big brother versus little brother. Due to land constraints in a sprawling urban area, the course was built as a spectacular inner-city executive course.

The holes weren't long (longest par-4 was around 320 yards), but the immense par-56 layout exhibited a crafty design. The key to scoring well on the front nine was pinpoint accuracy and placement, but to score well on the back nine, one would have to possess the uncanny knack to "attack." The back nine was unique. It gave golfers plenty of options to go pin seeking.

I remember the last round I played at the course with my dad back in 2005, when he was in the ATL visiting. It was one for the ages. He had always been one of the best putters that I had ever seen, but on this day he got extremely moist. He made the turn at 6 under par and had gotten it to 9 deep before we lost daylight and were forced to quit after 15 holes.

Dad was known for his consistency, and this was the third time in my golfing life that I had experienced him playing a round of unconscious golf. The other two times were in tournaments back in North Carolina. The most memorable came at the Crosby Pro-Am, which was held at Bermuda Run Country Club. He had gotten off to a good start and completed his round with an easy 8-under-par 64. Nice! Sam Puryear, Sr., my namesake, was my man. This round in the ATL was also incredibly special considering that several years later my dad lost his sight due to what we believe are several hereditary factors. That would be his final round of golf ever in Atlanta.

Now the humor and the insanity of the neighborhood championship continues. Shelton has won three bets with two presses, Brandon one and Willie and Rod none. Willie and Rod realize that the only way to even the score with this group is to press and win the last hole. They also realize today that their swings resemble more of a caddie swing with a hitch instead of the normal fluid golfer's motion. It doesn't matter. This will be their only true chance of throwing Shelton off his game and getting under his skin.

When describing the East Lake Junior Golf program to friends and family, I would always lament one key factor. These kids were "real" and transparent. They approached golf differently. They trash talked, got in your face, laughed at your bad shots, and encouraged you to miss putts. They brought a basketball and football mentality to the country club.

I have to admit, although it was different, it actually made the game a lot more appealing in many instances.

"Shelton…is that Quesha over there with DeDe?" quips Rod. The group breaks up in laughter. Shelton loves Quesha, but they are always on and off. DeDe is also a big punch line. DeDe is the neighborhood Casanova always trying to get with someone else's girl. He is a tall, lanky, blue-black-looking brother with a head full of naps.

Shelton laughs, but glances at Rod and says, "This shot is for my baby, Ms. Lowery. Rod, where is the security van." Shelton always retaliates with a joke about dating Rod's mom. They call her minivan a security van. It doesn't help that his mom is a part-time security guard.

This is the origin of Rod's mom's security van jokes: The boys and I had just returned from Bermuda. We had flown over to compete against the best juniors on the island. Since the Charlie Yates Golf Course was centrally located, we always used it to begin and end our golfing excursions. It essentially served as our safe haven for the parents, kinda like the Boys and Girls Club did for me back in the day. While waiting out front, Rod's mom (we called her Ms. Geraldine) was pulling up in a wagon, not just any wagon, but a 1990 Chrysler Plymouth van. The van had the brown plank-looking colors draping the outside. I am not sure how it passed its yearly inspections, but it did and it was old and it was raggedy. Preparing for her van was very similar to attending a NASCAR race at the Atlanta Motor Speedway. You would hear Ms. Geraldine's van coming before you could actually see her. The vehicle was loud. It sounded like a mix of a lawn mower and a 747 taking off. We also called her van the paddy wagon (police term).

As the paddy wagon was about to stop in front of the clubhouse, the engine literally died at the front door. A large plume of smoke escaped out of the back pipes. After about 35 minutes of trying to figure out what to do, eight of us had to strategically position ourselves to push the heavy van out of the pick-up lanes. Ms. Geraldine now really had a dilemma. She didn't have a AAA card, nor any money to call a tow truck. This is when she began to improvise. When she popped her trunk, we thought she was going to get a car jack and some tools, but we realized she had a trunk full of candy apples in the back and she was about to try to make some money. We were dumbfounded. We watched in amazement for about two hours. We thought she was simply coming to pick up Rod, but this seemed too planned and too rehearsed. Ms. Geraldine was the neighborhood candy and snack lady. She was always finding ways to make a few bucks. So what do you think?

With all of the jokes flowing during this round of golf, Shelton tries to buckle down and get back to business. He stands over his shot. Shelton is facing a downhill 205-yard shot with the pin tucked in the back right corner. A nice inviting bunker protects the center of the green, which is the normal bail-out area for the chickenhearted. Shelton pulls a 6-iron from his bag and plays a nice butter cut fade. The hole plays to Shelton's natural shot shape, which is left to right. The ball lands about 12 feet right of the pin, but with the spin it ends up five feet from the stick, leaving him with a short putt for birdie.

Now the game is really on. Everyone on the tee box continues to laugh and joke about each other's momma, their shade of black melanin, their weight, and their freaky sisters. The craziness intensifies.

Brandon and Willie play their normal shot shape (which is a strong draw, a close cousin to a strong hook) and both end up with 25-foot and 27-foot putts respectively. Rod tries to go for the gusto and leaves it short in the bunker. I honestly never thought Rod ever considered the difficulty on any shot. He gathered his number, pulled his club, and swung. Hell, I would bet dollars to donuts that half the time Rod probably never knew any correct distances. The old saying of paralysis by analysis didn't apply to Rod.

Now, considering his terrible bunker game and the lack of data, he is definitely staring bogey or double bogey in the face.

After only a couple more shots, the hole will be over.

As the boys begin walking up on the green, they start to notice a small group of people gathering in the parking lot. The parking lot at the Charlie Yates Golf Course faces the 18th green. These folks are all dressed in crisp blue uniforms and they seem to be systematically loading up on carts. From a distance, the kids can't decipher who is who, but they see a lot of movement. The 18th green faces the clubhouse. Based on the elevation of the hole, the 18th green provides a panoramic shot of the entire neighborhood. Since it's the highest point on the golf course, it makes for an incredible vantage point to take in downtown Atlanta.

Brandon laughs.... "Why is the po-po getting on carts?"

"They are coming out here to gamble like everybody else," says Willie. "Them fools don't have any clubs and they are probably broke as hell."

Shelton starts laughing and jokes, "They are driving over here. I am surprised Ms. Lowery isn't with them." Now the laughter is out of control. He continues, "Hey, Willie, they are coming to get you for selling bootleg CDs up at the BP." Willie was notorious for selling bootleg CDs around the neighborhood.

And then the unthinkable happens.

The laughter quickly stops.

Eight officers walk up on the green, paired up, announce themselves and their intentions, and proceed to arrest Willie and Brandon. "Johnny Po-Po" reads them their rights and they haul them off to the Dekalb County Jail.

What the what? Crazy! What just happened?

Everyone is dumbfounded and befuddled, but more importantly, Willie and Brandon just got locked up.

This book was written not only for Shelton, Willie, Brandon, Rod, JB, Eric, and the slew of others who grew up in the neighborhood "Little Vietnam," which is what East Lake Meadows was so aptly nicknamed, but for the myriad of other parents and young people around the United States who have and are constantly striving to make a better life for themselves with the paucity of resources that they have been dealt. This is a story of transformation. This neighborhood experiment has served as a model of redemption in cities like Washington D.C, Charlotte, New Orleans, and Denver, to name a few. This model has helped change public housing and the expectations and connotations associated with it. These cities have taken very challenged neighborhoods and refurbished the concrete and the people from the inside out. The local schools in these communities embraced the charter school concept, the self-sufficiency model or employment for the parents, and innovative methods to improve the overall health of the neighborhoods.

The book highlights the past 20-plus years of what started off as a unique golf story, but has now evolved into a true human-interest masterpiece.

More importantly, this story defines God's presence and his hand in all of our lives.

The story of these young people is a powerful adaptation of the beauty and puissance of God's kingdom. This book was written to encourage faith, inspiration, and perseverance. This is the hope of an incredible group of people who developed patience and a strong belief system through one of the most positive and impactful neighborhood transformational stories in the history of urban development. These kids are winners and they made it. Their victory or successes is pyric in many ways, but global in scope.

These families experienced some personal successes, despite their challenges. The human element is the hidden ingredient in the revitalization. Growing up in a tough, crime-ridden environment, being black and stereotyped, was only a small part of the narrative. Traditional data under normal circumstances would have indicated that this equation wasn't possible. Some of the data points were correct. A few of the youth in the Atlanta neighborhood did fall short of my hopes and dreams for them. I saw myself as kind of a father figure to most of them. Several girls had babies at young ages, some kids quit school, and some were incarcerated. I am convinced that with the creation of a few more band-aids in their lives, both the real or imagined wounds could have been treated.

The children were always told about the light at the end of the tunnel, but I am afraid that many of the folks in the streets thought the light represented a train.

This was an area where most of the young black boys and girls wore braids or dreads. This was a community where white tees and long, baggy shorts were the accepted attire. This was a neighborhood where there were more pay phones, which were used for illegal activities, than there were fathers. The average parent in the community didn't have a high school education. The educational system had completely turned its back on this community. Crime was as prevalent as the delivery of mail.

On my first day on the job at East Lake, I met the neighborhood mailman, Jerry. Jerry came inside our house/office to deliver our mail. He was laughing when he said people randomly search mailboxes and steal the mail at the first of the month. The government always sends out checks at the beginning of every month.

Jerry was a tall and thick dude. He looked at me and said, "Hey, you must be new."

I smiled and asked, "Why do you say that?"

He said I'd find out. He started chuckling. I noticed that he wore the normal postal blue shorts and long blue socks. Jerry had already helped himself to a couple of the cold apple juices in the fridge. Thirsty ass! The office kept the fridge stocked with soda and juice. It seriously felt like I was working from the crib. I definitely didn't have any excuse not to be hydrated.

On his way out the door, he turned and said, "Welcome to the neighborhood," but then he did something I will never forget. He raised his shirt and showed me the 9mm handgun that he carried in his waistband. He said, "I don't leave home without it." I was startled, to say the least. I was thinking this wasn't the American Express commercial of "Don't leave home without it" that I had heard before.

He finished up by telling me a couple of stories about delivering mail in East Lake. He said, "You know they call this place Little Vietnam." I shook my head no, because this was news to me.

He said working in the neighborhood was like being out on the battlefield. Jerry had done a 15-month tour in Afghanistan. There was only one way to enter and only one way to exit the neighborhood. He said delivering checks at the first of the month was seriously like being on active duty.

The mismanagement of funds, the overflow of welfare recipients, the $100 million neighborhood drug trade, and the abundance of birthing children for a check all added to the dysfunction.

Then he looked at me and winked. As he walked out, he threw up the peace sign (deuces) and said "be careful" and "you better make friends with the residents."

I worked in the neighborhood for nine years, and it was perhaps the best nine years of my working life. I was fortunate enough to be involved in a deluge of decisions and actions that will arguably go down as one of the greatest redevelopment stories in the history of gentrification. This is truly what the neighborhood was…a gentrification experiment.

Shelton Davis, Willie Brown, Rod Lowery, Brandon Bradley, JB Holsey, Eric Davis, Travis Leslie, and Brandon Greene are only a few of my success stories. They are not alone coming from the neighborhood, but they definitely endured and achieved. I viewed each young person as a tree. All trees eventually grow branches, leaves, and sometimes fruit.

Leviticus 23:40 says:

"And you shall take on the first day the fruit of splendid trees, branches of palm trees and boughs of leafy trees and willows of the brook, and you shall rejoice before the Lord your God seven days."

Based on the experiences of these young folks, the fruit coming from their trees will now have more of an opportunity to develop and grow. They manipulated their personal narratives and these are their stories.

CHAPTER 2

The Story of East Lake

"I am the Lord your God, Who brought you out of the
land of Egypt; Open your mouth wide, and I will fill it."

(Psalm 81:10)

The East Lake neighborhood has a storied history. This was the home of
Bobby Jones, Charlie Yates, and Alexa Stirling, three of the most highly
decorated amateur golfers of all time. East Lake is located about 10 miles
east of downtown Atlanta.

During the early 1900s, East Lake was a wonderful retreat for the
Atlanta elite. Coca-Cola executives and their families and most of the
wealthy major-industry bigwigs maintained a presence in the community.

Although close to downtown, it was a lot like country living.
A beautiful country club, with two courses and a lake located in a
picturesque motif of fashion.

The neighborhood seemed to have it all.

And then it happened…

The 1950s and early 1960s brought about what the government
coined "white flight." White flight was described as the move of white
city-dwellers to the suburbs, to escape the influx of minorities. The
suburbs were attractive. The suburbs were developing into mini-cities

with emerging shopping malls, new schools, and sprawling subdivisions. Residents were also attracted to the large, treesy lots with newfound fresh air. New cars and new highways allowed them the ability to drive from the suburbs to downtown quickly. The city of Atlanta lost more than 100,000 residents to its northern neighbors. These new surroundings created a new, more diverse neighborhood within the East Lake community. There were no similarities. The new normal consisted of a government-assisted housing community, no financial institutions, no grocery stores or dry cleaners, and a new school with no windows. The crime rate became one of the worse in the state. Drugs and aggressive crimes became a regular occurrence. The neighborhood averaged two assaults per week.

One out of every four residents were victims of a violent crime. The neighborhood operated a multimillion-dollar-a-year drug trade. The average family income was less than $10,000 a year. Less than one in 30 households had a father living in the home. The community was a "hot" mess.

Many of the city leaders and most of the residents had essentially ignored the area.

The irony in all of this bedlam was its spectacular epicenter of championship golf. East Lake Golf Club was situated in the center of this foolishness. The famed history of the golf club along with its pristine location was unheralded. I equate it to the notorious San Quentin State Prison, which is located off the coast of San Francisco. The facility has many of the best scenic views on the West Coast, but it housed some of the worst convicts in the country.

There was one caveat:

The property values plummeted. The course, which had once been a hub for major championship golf, had spiraled into a tsunami of disrepair. Due to socioeconomic pendulum shifts, the course had literally tried to separate itself from the "new" neighborhood.

East Lake Golf Club had placed an ugly green tarp up on the property fencing surrounding the course.

The goal was to make the course invisible from the outside world. It worked! The course had now become a "ghetto Camelot."

The out-of-sight, out-of-mind concept was in full effect. My aunt and uncle, who live up the street on Candler Road, told me one afternoon that they had never seen what the inside of the course looked like. They had never seen what was inside the fence. The discolored green tarp essentially made you forget that a golf course was even present. The course had also become a literal hazard. I don't mean sand traps, out of bounds stakes, and lakes, but a "living safely" hazard. Several of the golf holes butted up next to a few streets (Glenwood, Alston, and Second). The street access created a new source of community income. A really bad and dangerous kind.

Many of the golfers began meeting many of their unscrupulous neighbors who were not very neighborly. They carried guns. Many of these criminals had figured out the secret and shortcut to a quick payday. They jumped the canvas-covered fences that bordered the course, brandished guns, and regularly stole whatever they could carry.

East Lake Golf Club was also just a pitching wedge away from Memorial Drive. Memorial Drive was full of history. The irony is that the road heads north from the golf course and dead ends at Stone Mountain Park. Stone Mountain is famous because of the carvings etched into its monstrous structure. The structure depicts three figures of the Confederate States of America: Stonewall Jackson, Robert E. Lee, and Jefferson Davis. Stone Mountain also gained notoriety because of its mention in Dr. Martin Luther King, Jr's "I Have a Dream" speech. Dr. MLK, Jr. knew the significance of his words: Stone Mountain was the normal marching and meeting spot for the Ku Klux Klan.

The city of Atlanta started to expand and change. The population started to explode. Dr. Martin Luther King, Jr. was leading marches, and the rights of "coloreds" were at least coming across television sets around the country.

Blacks began moving out of downtown Atlanta. Based on the proximity from downtown, the East Lake neighborhood was one of the closest destinations to the city center. This served as a major landing area for blacks.

The Board of Directors and the persons governing East Lake Country Club sold the facility. They didn't want any part of the new normal. They moved out to the northern suburbs and developed the Atlanta Athletic Club.

A lot of people didn't and don't realize that East Lake Country Club consisted of two championship courses. The country club was initially owned by the Atlanta Athletic Club and they built the first course on the property in 1908. It was also the site of an amusement park, which surrounded the current lake on the property. The AAC built the second course, which they called the No. 2 course, in 1930. This was actually a really special year for the club. Bobby Jones won the British Amateur Championship match on May 31, 1930, the year he became the first and only man to win the Grand Slam of Golf (United States Amateur, United States Open, British Amateur, and British Open).

The courses were spectacular and were full of a lot of memories, but had become dispensable due to the change of the economic narrative. The decision was made by the AAC membership to dispose of one course and keep the other. They decided to sell the No. 2 course to developers. The land was sold and eventually became associated with the Atlanta Housing Authority. The AAC moved north to Duluth, Georgia, and built a really swanky and impressive new Atlanta Athletic Club. According to many historians, the remnants or owned land that remained allowed the neighborhood to go to hell in a handbasket. When you take the strong economic backing out of any neighborhood in America, you are depleting the neighborhood at its most vital point. The neighborhood and the entire area fell on tough times.

It is amazing that in many places in our "great" nation, the pervasive thought remains paramount that certain hues of skin types are bad for their property values and their children's education. It's also funny that the negative mindset in America that existed in the '80s is still prevalent in today's divisive America.

Following "white flight," the rise of bedlam, and now a renewed vision, the East Lake area is now the primary home to gentrification and a racially diverse population. The only consistency has been golf. Golf had given the neighborhood recognition and fame for its white occupants, and now it would do the same thing on the same fertile ground for the blacks in the area. In the Bible, in the book of Matthew, Jesus said, "He that soweth the good seed is the Son of man; the field is the world; the good seed are the children of the kingdom." The seeds eventually sprouted, and the new design has God's imprint all over it.

CHAPTER 3

My Move to Atlanta

"Trust in the Lord with all your heart, and do not lean on
your own understanding. In all your ways acknowledge
him and he will make straight your paths."

(Proverbs 3:5-6)

I accepted the job at East Lake because I loved Atlanta and I had family
in the area. The job consisted of teaching golf, creating programming that
would integrate academics and golf, fundraising, recruiting volunteers,
developing volunteer structure, hosting junior events, and developing
any opportunities that would benefit the youth through the game of golf.
The other attractive component to the position was the promise to allow
me to utilize all of my skills and creativity to actively impact an area
with my two favorite passions, which were working with young people
and advancing the game of golf. I had played golf in college at Tennessee
State University in Nashville from 1988 to 1992. I had grown up in a
junior golf program in Winston-Salem, North Carolina. My passions
were clearly developed at a really early age.

I realized a long time ago what golf meant to me. My father had been a
small college All-American at Winston Salem State University in 1965.
Many of our family friends and our family trips were created because of

the game of golf. It was simply something we did. More importantly for me was its purpose. It served as an outlet, which allowed me to spend more time with my dad. I wanted to emulate him. He was my role model.

Internally, I felt the job at East Lake would be an opportunity for me to effectively impact and positively change lives. I have always believed God leads us in everything we do. God directs our thoughts and rules our minds and hearts. I thought of this as a legacy changer. I also felt as though this would be an extension of my parents. My mom was a teacher/professor and my dad a high school principal. They had given their lives to making a difference. I honestly wanted to do the same thing.

Accepting the job was also about timing. One day earlier I had flown to New Orleans to interview and subsequently received an offer to work for the Boy Scouts of America in the New Orleans council. I asked them to give me three days. I flew back home, repacked, and boarded another plane, but this time, headed to Atlanta for the East Lake interview.

In hindsight the selection of East Lake was a great decision. Years later Hurricane Katrina really affirmed the decision. On August 23, 2005, Katrina ravaged the Gulf Coast, causing $108 billion worth of damage and killing 1,833 people. New Orleans was literally underwater. God had truly spared me because being in the midst of the destruction would have really altered my life.

East Lake was a pillar of figurative destruction. This is a truly *sui generis* story of transformation. There are not many business leaders let alone many business entities that could have pulled off the neighborhood development miracle. I am convinced there is only one person in Atlanta who could have initiated the spark. The guy with the dream and the vision was Tom Cousins. Everyone has an incredible story to tell, but Mr. Cousins' story is truly remarkable.

CHAPTER 4

Tom Cousins

"It is easier for a camel to go through the eye of a needle than for a rich man to enter the kingdom of God."

(Mark 10:25)

Tom Cousins, a devout Christian, often spoke about his vision for the East Lake community. The conversations about changing lives and giving people opportunities and dreams seamlessly struck a chord with the Greater Atlanta area and the national golf community. It really disturbed him that the educational system in the area was one of the worst in the city of Atlanta.

Cousins read a *New York Times* article in 1993 that essentially stated the New York prison system was at least 70 percent occupied by eight New York neighborhoods. Cousins was interested in these statistics and asked the law enforcement officials in Atlanta if the same statistics would be true in Georgia and more importantly in the city of Atlanta. After doing the research, the city officials mentioned that the statistics were true, but professed that the number of neighborhoods was not eight; it was less than four. East Lake Meadows, the housing projects in the East Lake neighborhood, was identified as the worst.

Many of the students I worked with over the years confided that they slept in bathtubs many nights to prevent getting hit by stray bullets coming through the walls. Families kept a plethora of unregistered firearms in the houses for protection. According to the crime statistics of the day, 90 percent of the residents of East Lake Meadows were victims of a felony. The drug industry was the largest neighborhood business trade. The average age of a grandmother in the neighborhood was 32 years old. The most alarming statistic was educationally based. In the neighborhood, only five percent of the qualifying fifth-graders were capable of passing the state's math test.

Tom Cousins was a remarkable businessman, but one of his recreational loves was playing golf. Mr. Cousins grew up idolizing Bobby Jones, the greatest amateur golfer of all time. One day, while enjoying a reception at the Stirling House, a house that Mr. and Mrs. Cousins purchased, Mr. Cousins revealed the true purity of his neighborhood heart. The Stirling House was the remodeled house that Alexia Stirling and her family owned when she was growing up. Stirling was one of the greatest female amateur golfers of her era, which was during the early to mid-1900s. Stories around the East Lake neighborhood have often discussed some of the famed matches between Stirling and Jones, with Stirling winning several of them.

The location of the house is also very strategic. It is actually located across from the 1st tee box at East Lake Golf Club. It was also located in the center of the redevelopment. The house served as the perfect abode when guests such as Sean Connery, Dave Pelz, Sid Matthews, and many other celebrities needed to relax and spend an evening before partaking in a magical round of golf at East Lake.

Mr. Cousins had amassed his fortune as a real estate developer. In Atlanta, his company Cousins Properties developed CNN Center, the Bank of America building, Frost Bank Tower, EQ Office, 191 Peachtree Tower, Omni Coliseum, and Emory Point to only name a small percentage of their genius. These development efforts helped shape the Atlanta skyline. He was also a huge sports enthusiast. He was responsible for bringing the Atlanta Hawks to Atlanta in 1968 from St.

Louis. He was also the owner of the Atlanta Flames of the NHL. He sold them to a group in Calgary in 1980. His purchase of East Lake Golf Club definitely fell in line with his core beliefs and values.

During this reception at the Stirling House, Tom shared something powerful.

He said, "Sam, people are trying to say that with all of my work, I am trying to buy my way into heaven. Well, you know what the 'good book' says. 'It is easier for a camel to go through the eye of a needle than for a rich man to enter the kingdom of God.' (Mark 10:25)

"I guess I am, but is anything wrong with that?" He continued, "Is there anything wrong with people that have a little more than others sharing it with those that don't have anything?" Mr. Cousins made me a believer.

CHAPTER 5

Walking into the Church

"He must become greater; I must become less."

(John 3:30)

The journey through East Lake was a great one. When I first arrived in Atlanta in January 1998, I drove to a growing, nearby church, not too far from the golf course. The church was the site of ELJGA. I had been hired as the executive director of the East Lake Junior Golf Academy. I was responsible for overseeing the administration, programs, and strategic plan for the junior golf program. A few of my other duties included fundraising, marketing, and community outreach. I reported to the East Lake Community Foundation and its Board of Directors. The church was actually located in a great spot. It was located directly beside Highway I-20, next to a gas station, one mile from two golf courses, within three miles of several elementary and middle schools, within a mile of the YMCA, and best of all, right next to the main Marta line. In Atlanta, the Marta is very important for a lot of folks. The joke if you live there is that Marta stands for "Moving African-Americans Rapidly

Through Atlanta." The public transportation system is not as good as it is in the average big city, but it is what it is.

I walked into a room in the church and felt like I was immediately engulfed in a time warp. I stood facing 30 students in an after-school program. Their faces appeared young in age, but worn with life experiences.

Their faces all depicted a story. Most of these children were a part of what mainstream America commonly defines as "dysfunctional." How does "mainstream" America define dysfunction?

Some of their parents were incarcerated; some were junkies; and some were battling depression. None of their parents had college degrees. Most of the parents didn't work. This is America's definition. It isn't accurate, but it is the "America" that has traditionally described and defined our undervalued inner cities.

One by one, I introduced myself to each child. It also hit home with me that most of these children had been hurt or lied to by a variety of outside program entities that had tried to come into the community promising hope and change. Creating programs and targeting these communities had become chic by folks vying to make a quick buck. According to Eva Davis, a community activist, these groups indeed got paid, but with poor structural components and programming and insouciant beliefs and care for their constituents, they left a trail of carnage and deceit in the neighborhood. But they weren't the only shortcomings in the community. The fatherless void was real. It also hit home that out of the 450 families living in the "Meadows" only 16 households had fathers living in the house. The school in the middle of the hood was void of windows. In many private circles, it was said that the school was built for the "project" children and no one else. It was a way to keep them together. In laymen terms this is how the CDC treats germs and diseases; they isolate them and treat them in a vacuum.

Their response to me was mixed. Some sneered; some commented amongst themselves. Some of them amusingly sucked their lips and mumbled under their breath. The indifferent responses were perfect. It was exactly what the doctor ordered. It really got my juices flowing and it also exacerbated that there was a really important job to do in the community. The new constituents were going to have to believe the best was around the corner.

My commitment was to create and foster their dreams. I was going to make a believer out of my new flock. Mr. Sam, which is what I was most commonly called by the neighborhood, was the new sheriff in town. My innate commitment also meant that in order to see this goal rise to fruition, I was going to have to sacrifice a lot of personal family time. In my mind, accepting the job now meant I had overnight increased the size of my family by tenfold. I now had 40-plus children to worry about, including my personal three who lived with me.

These kids were typical. Some were inquisitive about my past. Some wondered how long I would be there. Most of the children and families in the program were oblivious to the financials; therefore, they assumed I wouldn't be there long, since I was working or volunteering for free. This is also a socio-economic norm.

This was an instant realization that a "neighborhood perception" paradigm of outsiders coming to help had to positively change. I vowed to do anything and everything to help improve their lives.

I also told anyone who would listen that if East Lake brought me in to serve as a babysitter, they were in for a rude awakening. I was drawing a line in the sand. I was willing to creatively nudge the powers at East Lake to help assist and empower the people in the community. Janie Stratigos, my supervisor at the time, told me that they didn't have a succinct blueprint for my position. She mentioned that if I were able to do what was on my resume in the community, then the young people would definitely greatly benefit. My role was to create exposure and provide opportunities. I was hired to serve as a golf instructor and fundraising executive, but I think they also received a life coach who wasn't afraid to dream.

CHAPTER 6

My Upbringing

"He who spares his rod hates his son, but he who loves him disciplines him promptly."

(Proverbs 13:24)

The first time I went to the golf course with Shelton and Eric Davis, Willie, and Rod, a weird thing happened.

I honestly looked at these kids as the persons who they were capable of becoming. I have never been able to answer the conundrum of why those kids. I just instantly became interested in their denouement. I liked them and I guess they liked me.

My relationship with these boys, who were nine and 10 years old at the time, was forged on the first day we hit the golf course. I had a nice mix of boys and girls. I realized a few things on that first day that would become very helpful in guiding me through the process of trying to save lives.

This group shared a lot of similarities. Their mothers played an integral role. The boys and girls, who ranged from ages seven to 13, were from low-income families. The kids were active in other sports. The blessing in the mire was the respect level. All of these boys were very respectful children. I was always taught by my parents that people are indeed rich and blessed in so many ways. Their smiles and their high levels of respect made these children pharaohs in their creative neighborhood fiefdoms.

My initial style of golf was definitely different than your average. I centered the entire teaching concept on life skills and dreams. I often told the kids that golf was "the only true game of life." I also approached golf from one basic perspective. I wanted every child to enjoy coming to the golf course, and I wanted the game to be fun. My motto was following the acronym KISMIF. This stands for Keep It Simple, Make It fun.

This is how the game was introduced to me at six years old. I shared a name with my father. I was a junior and he was a senior, but as time waned, I also developed his passion for the game.

Both of my parents attended Winston-Salem Teachers College—now Winston-Salem State University (WSSU) in Winston-Salem, North Carolina—and each received their degrees in education. They continued their education and received master's degrees and many other professional certifications from neighboring institutions (UNC, North Carolina A&T, Appalachian State). My upbringing prepared me for this opportunity.

There are a lot of things you can learn through experience that you can't learn from a textbook. My dad was one of 11 children and my mother was one of four. I grew up listening to stories about very difficult financial times, but incredibly loving times. My parents often talked about the redundancy of challenges that confronted them on a regular basis, but the one common theme in both of their lives was love and respect.

When my dad caddied and brought home 60 cents a day from the golf course, he shared it with his mother. No one complained about sharing one bathtub full of water with your siblings. No one complained about cutting wood for the fireplace. No one complained about sharing food at mealtime. In all honesty if they had complained, they would have probably gotten knocked out. Life was difficult, but life was difficult for most blacks during the mid- to late '40s and early '50s.

I listened to stories about drinking from different water fountains (one for colored people and one for whites). I also heard the stories about the ridiculous treatment blacks received at the local golf courses. The treatment was not good. These stories actually pissed me off as a kid. Blacks were good enough to carry some racist clown's golf bag, but not good enough to play on the course. In some cities, municipalities built "black" golf courses (poorly maintained areas of unkept land) to essentially appease or placate the blacks who wanted to play the game.

But the one common thread was the value of a great education. Education was priceless and timeless! Education was the only true railroad to freedom.

The historically black universities (HBCU) served as a hub for America's brightest blacks. It gave them hope for their futures, and it helped prepare them to make a difference in their neighborhoods and communities. The fact that my father played golf at WSSU and received Small College All-American status in 1965 was very unusual. Many years later my dad was inducted into the WSSU Hall of Fame.

Most of the blacks who had been exposed to golf during this era and the ones preceding it had been exposed to golf through the caddie ranks. I previously mentioned that whites actually thought they were doing blacks a favor by letting them carry their bags. But caddying did a lot more for blacks in the game of golf than people initially realized. It actually provided a steady income for a lot of young black boys at courses around the country and especially in the South. It also gave them limited access to play. Most courses designated at least one day during the week for caddies to play golf.

During slavery, blacks weren't allowed to read. Blacks stayed up late at night and snuck around because they realized the importance of the written word. Caddies did the same thing through the game of golf. Caddies would sneak a club out of a golfer's bag or, in a lot of cases, they would take clubs that no one else wanted. The grooves would be worn out or the grips would be worn. The iron faces were as smooth as spoons. The black caddies would take the groove-less irons and get a hatchet, and with the help of a hammer create new grooves. The grooves were important for ball flight and spin. These newly created grooves would make a ball dance, but totally destroy the ball with their jagged edges.

These caddies would learn how to use one club. They would master and perfect that one club. They would learn a myriad of shots. They became scientists within the game of golf due to the constant experimentation with the one stick. This would eventually lead them to creatively develop an entire set of matchstick clubs. This set would include several different brands. MacGregor and Spalding irons, Hogan wedges, and Powerbilt woods were the popular equipment choices during the 1960s. These were only a few of the lessons learned from my parents.

My father had led a WSSU squad from 1961 to 1965. His Rams teams won four CIAA Conference championships. He never lost a match. At the time he was peaking, the crosstown beacon in the golf world, Wake Forest University, was also producing All-Americans. The WSSU golfers and their stories never made it to print. The WFU golfers regularly made it to the front page and eventually created history with their accomplishments.

The world was slowly getting acclimated to a cadre of blacks challenging the times and trying to make their living out on tour. Charlie Sifford, Teddy Rhodes, Charlie Owens, Lee Elder, James Black, and Pete Brown, just to name a few, had developed great reputations on the "Chitlin' Circuit" (which is what the black tour was called). They were finding a slew of obstacles trying to play mainstream golf. A Boston dentist, Dr. George Grant, invented the modern golf tee. Teddy Rhodes became the second black man to play in the U.S. Open, in 1948. Ann Gregory was the first black woman to play in the U.S. Women's Amateur, in 1956. Lee Elder became the first black player to compete in the famed Masters Tournament. Charlie Sifford became the first black man to play a regular schedule of events on the PGA Tour.

In 1963 Althea Gibson became the first black woman to compete on the LPGA Tour. She was an incredible athlete. She also competed in and won tennis's Wimbledon and the U.S. Nationals (precursor to the U.S. Open) twice (1957, 1958). She was also the first black player to win a Grand Slam title in tennis with her French Open victory in 1956. I am also proud to say that I watched her play at my home course in Winston-Salem when I was a teenager in the 1980s. She played with Al

Wood (UNC basketball great and former NBA player), Jim Thorpe, and Chuck Thorpe. It is a day I will never forget. Many years later I would meet Al on a golf course in Charlotte and ask him about that special day.

Pete Brown became the first black man to win a PGA-sanctioned event. Calvin Peete won 12 times on the PGA Tour, and his career culminated with a great Ryder Cup performance. Tiger Woods became the first black man to win the Masters. As of this writing, he has won 82 career PGA Tour events, which has him tied with Sam Snead for the most career victories.

I would later become the first black man to serve as a head collegiate golf coach at a Power Five Conference institution. Regardless of the oblivious nature of the world, black people have truly made a huge impact on the game of golf. I am simply glad that my dad gave me a set of keys and the opportunity to open the specific doors within the game that I deemed necessary for my future.

The times were very intense for a young black man trying to play professional golf. My father knew he didn't have the financial backing. He also realized that a regular paycheck was a non-negotiable. These beliefs forced him to dash all of his professional golf playing hopes and dreams. After graduating from college, he married my mother, took a job as a teacher in Wilson, North Carolina, in 1965, and earned a fat amount of $6,500 per year. LMAO

My father taught me a lot of the necessary fundamentals of the game, but more importantly, he taught me more about life. I always hoped that I had the opportunity to one day share a lot of what was instilled in me with others.

I grew up emulating my father. I wanted to make better grades, be a better golfer, and be as kind and financially generous to others as my father was to the world. I only had one sibling, which was my brother Eric. I wanted to serve as a positive role model for him. He was only eight years old when I went to college and I knew he watched my every move.

CHAPTER 7

TSU

"If service, in our serving; the one who teaches,
in his teaching..."

(Romans 12:7)

My experiences at TSU were wonderful, but I had made my mind up when I got there to place golf on the map. The history of TSU was good, but the athletic history of TSU was awesome. Wilma Rudolf, Richard Dent, "Jefferson Street" Joe Gilliam, Claude Humphrey, Coach Ed Temple, Ed "Too Tall" Jones, 17 Olympic gold medals, Wyomia Tyus, Edith McGuire, Barbara Jones, Lucinda Williams, Mae Faggs, Ralph Boston, Madeline Manning, Willye White, Kathy McMillan, Chandra Cheeseborough, Anthony Pleasant, Tony Stargell, Jim Marsalis, Larry Kinnebrew, Carlos Rogers, and Anthony Mason were some of the athletic legends. Don't let me forget the iconic Oprah Winfrey. Although she wasn't an athlete, she is the most famous of them all.

I wanted to place golf in the long lineage of special athletic literature at TSU. Although athletics were king at TSU, golf was different. We didn't get the respect nor the love from the big sports, actually from any sports. We didn't get much love period. It had become a common joke to many of my classmates who said they wish they would have paid more attention to the game of golf back then because they are addicted to the game now as adults.

The golf team at TSU carried about 10 players. We wore interesting outfits. When I reference interesting, I really mean colorful. Coach dressed us like we were members of the black Jack and Jill organization. Trust me...these were not your normal golf outfits. With a female coach, I knew we would be clean, but our outfits skirted the line. Dayyyuuummmm...and the colors! Coach didn't believe in the basic colors. We wore mauve, coral, and pink along with the normal red, white, and blue. The mauve, coral, and pink concerned me because I perceived them as girly colors, but I never complained because we were at least uniformed.

The team participated in the Ohio Valley Conference. Playing in the OVC was controversial because it pretty much depleted the universities' natural black college rivalries. TSU was the only historically black institution in the conference. Schools such as Murray State, Middle Tennessee State University, Morehead State, Austin Peay, Southeast Missouri, and Tennessee Tech were several of the teams in the conference. Although I don't know the numbers, I am not convinced that TSU made a great business decision. Football is the bread and butter of the university. With the annihilation of the football rivalries, the move to the OVC seems to have been a killer. The move created homecoming football games against teams like Morehead State and Southeast Missouri rather than HBCU favorites like Grambling, Jackson State, and Central State.

Dr. Catana Starks was our fearless leader. She was the only female head coach of a Division I men's golf program in the country. She started a trend. As of 2019, there were 10 female coaches leading men's programs. Although we played in some really good tournaments, Coach experienced her share of troubles with the university. In the beginning, the university would stress her out and not pay her for months. This was tough on her. We unintentionally destroyed her car, since she was driving us to practice every day.

Can you imagine four or five big guys riding in a small blue Toyota Tercel every day? We were traveling from Nashville to Houston to

Tallahassee to Daytona. We were road warriors. We ate at Shoney's about 1,000 times during my four-year career; hence, this is why I don't visit Shoney's or any other restaurant resembling this style of service. In fact when I became a coach, I would take my team to the Golden Corral as a punishment when I felt as though they were being ungrateful. The GC Palace (my special name for Golden Coral) would always bring my guys back down to earth.

We drove more than 80,000 miles in a 15-passenger van, ate some delectable, mouth-watering meals, and wore some elegant, sophisticated-looking outfits, but the four years playing golf for the "Big Blue" were four of the best years of my life.

Coach and I didn't always see eye to eye, but I knew she cared about me as a person. It was bigger than golf. My experience with Coach also showed me that my biggest compliment to the game shouldn't be as a professional player. My largest contribution should be working with young people and creating a path in the coaching arena. I really wanted to impact the grassroots trajectory. If you don't teach and reach them early, you will never create more professionals. The game needed an injection from within. These were lessons I learned from my folks, but were reiterated at TSU. I have always been taught never to simply comment or complain about a problem. If it bothers you that much, get up and do something about it. Make a difference. Realize that God is in control and set out to serve.

As I sit here today and write, I am smiling thinking about our latest homecoming at TSU. I worked with Teresa Phillips, the athletic director at TSU, on creating a lunch for Coach Starks. She has dementia now and she is actively fighting breast cancer. A lot of the players who played with me and after me attended. She meant a lot to us. The lunch for Coach served as a lighthearted roast. We told a lot of stories that I had actually forgotten. Based on the different classes represented at the lunch, some stories were also brand new to me. Regardless of where the program started, it was definitely better after Coach Starks left her imprint on it.

This was the legacy I wanted to leave in Atlanta. I wanted to leave it better than I'd found it.

All of my upbringing and lessons learned as a player served as the perfect recipe for changing lives in the East Lake neighborhood.

I always pondered about creative ways to help these children. But in all honesty, I probably filled a much-needed void in their lives. If I were an essay, my role was adding the correct punctuation, a few big words, and utilizing the proper transitions.

They essentially wanted to "be like Mr. Sam." My philosophy when dealing with children has always been positive.

Children deserve to be treated like premium unleaded gas. You will get out of them what you invest in them. You don't fill up a Pinto or a Yugo with premium unleaded. When you buy a luxury car, you are supposed to treat it like the car it is designed to be. I tried to treat every child like a luxury vehicle.

CHAPTER 8

Charlie

"And a harvest of righteousness is sown
in peace by those who make peace."

(James 3:18)

From the beginning, I showered all the children with love, promise, and hope. It was a tough love, but it was sincere, transparent, and honest. I remember having to ban some of the neighborhood children from hitting balls because they didn't obey the golf course rules. I remember not taking some of the kids to tournaments because their report cards showcased a few Ds and Fs. The majority of the children responded to trust. If a kid was hungry, I would get them something to eat. If they didn't understand their homework, I stepped in to help tutor.

My first personal goal after taking the job was to meet with each family. I promised each family in the neighborhood one thing: If they placed their faith in me, I would definitely do right by their kids. We were operating a year-round program. We made sure every student received snacks and drink. We also monitored their clothing and their lifestyles. We stepped in to purchase whatever items were necessary to assist the young people and their families. I told them that this was possible because I placed my faith in God. I knew God wouldn't forsake me, and

I constantly gave him all the glory for any and all of my opportunities.

Golf was fun. This special group of children was very competitive. It also meant a lot to them because now each of them would have more time to grow up together.

The program started on the practice area at East Lake Golf Club. We hit wedges and wedges and wedges. We spent a lot of time on fundamentals. We spent more time discussing life and talking about life, but we kept it fun.

One special ingredient that really helped me do my job came in the form of a person. His name was Charlie Harrison. Charlie called himself a volunteer, but in truth, Charlie was East Lake.

Charlie was a great fellow. He was a throwback. He and Tom Cousins were first cousins. He had helped start one of the local black banks. He was an older guy who reminded me of my past. The only difference is that Charlie was white and the old men at Winston Lake Golf Course in my hometown were black.

Many of the students in the program saw Charlie as a relic. Remember, the average age of a grandparent in the East Lake neighborhood was 32 years old. His age more than doubled their norm. He also had an incredible golf acumen, background, and prowess for the job. Charlie qualified for the U.S. Amateur 16 times (he commonly referred to this by its previous name, which was the National Amateur). He also won the Atlanta Amateur on 10 occasions, won the Atlanta Athletic Club Championship nine times, the Atlanta Country Club championship six times, the 1955 Southern Amateur, and the 1959 Georgia Amateur. He was also an alternate on the 1967 Walker Cup team and a quarterfinalist at the 1980 British Amateur. He was a local legend.

Charlie played at Georgia Tech and was a member of their Hall of Fame. He made it to the quarters in the British Amateur and played in a couple of Masters Tournaments. He is also a member of the Georgia Sports Hall of Fame. Charlie was a good father and husband, and those two attributes about him were my favorites. Many years ago, while at a Tiger Woods junior golf clinic in Birmingham, I really realized how far Charlie's wings spread throughout the golfing world. I was standing on the driving range watching Rod receive a golf lesson from Tiger Woods. A guy walked up to me and asked me about my relationship with East Lake and my relationship with Charlie Harrison. After we conversed for about 20 minutes, he said be sure to tell Charlie I said hello. I promised him I would. The guy was Jerry Pate, 1976 U.S. Open champion.

Even with all of the kudos and accolades in his background, he always remained humble. This humbleness reminded me of my roots. Working with Charlie and working at the golf course taught me a lot. I definitely developed an addiction to the game of golf. I learned how to respect my elders, but I was often reminded that people have to stand up for what is right. I learned the true value of an education, while watching the local neighborhood pros gripe about their "real" jobs. If I had been given a nickel for every time I was told to go to college, I would truly be a rich man. Charlie reminded me of these guys.

Charlie and I believed that children had a purpose and place, but there was a time and a place for everything. We also agreed on stern but fair discipline. We also had many spirited discussions about race. We were from different generations. We had also come from different financial corners. Charlie had a few coins in the bank. I was searching for a few. As Sam Sr. would say, I was the squirrel trying to find a nut.

These simple yet succinct reminders really helped me relate with the East Lake boys. The boys needed all of the above. Although they were wonderful children, they were a little rough around the edges. We constantly corrected their grammar, asked them to tuck in their shirts, encouraged a positive presence, reiterated the importance of school, and reinforced respect for self, family, and world. We tried to accomplish all of this under the aegis of having fun playing a sport on some well-kept grass.

CHAPTER 9

Brandon

"God is our refuge and strength, an ever-present help in trouble. Therefore we will not fear, though the earth give way and the mountains fall into the heart of the sea, though its waters roar and foam and the mountains quake with their surging."

(Psalm 46:1-3)

Brandon was a late arrival to the program. He didn't join with the initial neighborhood sign-up. The first day I met him changed the prospects of the program forever.

I typically arrived at the golf course pretty early on Saturday mornings. The actual program started at 10 a.m., but in the beginning I liked to get there by 8 a.m. This gave me plenty of time to set up, but more importantly, it gave me a chance to work on my game. I always believed that staying sharp gave me a slight edge because the kids in the program were gunning for me. They were getting bigger and hitting the ball a long way. I totally focused on my 125 yards game and in. I was taught that the man with the best approach game and short game was the man who could win all the money. I was determined to wear the grooves out of all of my wedges.

Well, on one particularly beautiful Saturday morning while hitting balls, I turned around and noticed a tall, slim, dark-skinned fellow walking behind the range carrying what appeared to be plastic grocery bags. He looked to be about 10 years old, but he also looked to be athletic.

For this community, people carrying groceries from the neighborhood grocery store was not unusual. The folks in the "hood" also cashed their checks up at Mr. Lee's corner store. There wasn't a bank in the neighborhood either.

The thing that caught my attention was the time. It was early in the morning, but it was really early for a young 10-year-old boy to have already concluded the grocery shopping for his mom. It actually spoke of a higher level of responsibility and stronger presence of discipline. This made me look at myself. I was taken aback; I began to ask myself if I would have been willing to go to the grocery store for my parents at 7 a.m. in the morning. I probably would've complained like hell all the way in both directions.

I stopped hitting balls and walked from the range to the street, which was about 15 yards. I said, "Hey, man! Where are you coming from?"

He quickly backed up my assumption and said, "The grocery store."

I quipped, "Do you play golf?"

He smirked and said no. I asked him why, and he laughed.

I said, "What? Do you think golf is for punks?"

He laughed again. I asked him if he thought he could hit a golf ball, and like everyone who has never played the game, he said yes. I laughed and said…yeah okay…we will see.

Before allowing him to hit, we talked about several of his closest buddies that were in the East Lake Junior Golf Academy program. His buddies Shelton, Eric, Rod, and Willie were some of my best players.

At this point, amazingly enough, we were the only two people on the range. The largest knock on the Charlie Yates Golf Course was the name recognition. People simply didn't seem to know a lot about the golf course. I never figured out why. The Yates course was built on the site of the old East Lake Country Club No. 2 course. The course seemed to be hiding in plain sight. Driving range balls were inexpensive and it was located less than a mile off a major highway artery, I-20. To make matters worse, it was one the best conditioned golf courses in the city, but yet the range was empty.

I gave Brandon a 7-iron out of my bag, and I got out of the way. Not knowing much about the golf swing, he set up to the ball in his own way and swung. He whiffed! He totally missed the ball.

He set up again to the ball to attempt another swing and the second swing yielded a different result. His second swing connected. This exercise in humbleness went on for about five minutes. After watching him have a fair amount of success, I stepped in and began to teach. To my surprise, he hit some pretty good shots.

I also began to study more about him than just his swing.

Brandon had something special. He was patient, observant, analytical, and very methodical. I began working on a simple set-up and a shoulder turn. Brandon insisted that he thought he could be a good player. He wanted to develop a great swing.

I observed many of his practice swings and actions. This led me to believe that he was probably a good student in school and that he probably enjoyed math. His concern for precision and angles was extremely evident.

Brandon and I spent nearly two hours on the range alone. "I thought golf was easy, but I was wrong. I remember trying to hit the ball but I kept missing," said Brandon. After we hit all of the balls, Brandon walked back over to his groceries that he had placed on the cart path.

He looked back and asked, "Can I come back on another day?"

I smiled and told him that he was now an official part of the program. Brandon has been coming to the golf course ever since. Years later, Brandon made me tear up when he told me, "I don't know where I would be if I hadn't met you." He told me that he appreciated me always taking care of everything. I took care of golf stuff, school things, and anything that he and the others needed help with.

"Mr. Sam, you were always there. You were like a father to me. You never made us do anything we didn't want to do, but you supported us in everything we did."

The fatherly assertions were great, but whenever a parental figure is absent, the luggage has to be placed somewhere. Something or someone has to help create the healthy balance in people's lives. This is never an easy task, but it is an essential task.

After meeting Brandon's father, I instantly realized I would be attached to Brandon forever. His dad was very articulate and intelligent but had fallen victim to the streets.

During my time on the range with Brandon, I noticed a very tall black guy riding on a young boy's BMX bike. He was at a distance, but I could tell he had positioned himself to see what I was doing.

The guy wasn't neatly groomed and, in all honesty, he made me a little uneasy. As Brandon walked away, this large figure approached me. Although I was a newcomer to the neighborhood, I had heard a lot of the war stories about the area. I had heard dozens of reasons why the neighborhood was called "Little Vietnam." The senseless violence, the $100 million-a-year drug trade, the blighted hopes and dreams had been told to me in a countless number of ways. All of this was quickly playing itself in my mind.

The guy rode up on me and introduced himself. He said, "Hey, what's up? My name is Terry." He asked if I was new to the area. I told him my story and he intently listened. He said, "I don't mean to bother you, but I like what I saw you doing." He told me that he had recently relocated to Atlanta from New York. He continued by telling me that he had been shot, cut, and incarcerated on more than one occasion. The scar on his face told me that he had been in some battles. He told me that he had done drugs. As I sat and listened, I was thinking, *Oh shit, what does he want with me?* I was thinking to myself, *If I have to fight this man, then I better hit him first.* He was bigger than me and he looked strong as hell.

And then the strangest thing happened. He said, "Thank you."

I asked, "For what?"

He said, "The kid you were working with on the field (he called the driving range a field) is my son." He said, "I never thought I would see my son ever play golf." He went on by saying his son didn't know he was even living in Atlanta. He said that he just didn't want his son to grow up to be like him. He wanted Brandon to have a huge chance at a successful life. Brandon had four siblings, most of whom had some sort of criminal record.

Several years later there was an incident in East Lake that could have changed the course of Brandon's life. Although his family was forced to leave the neighborhood, I kept him close and worked with him on a daily basis. The odd part is that after the day I met him, I didn't see Brandon's dad again for years.

On one unassuming night, two intruders approached and opened fire on the family's apartment in the neighborhood. Joseph Bradley, one of Brandon's older brothers, hid the family behind the furniture upstairs. He grabbed a couple of the automatic weapons that were kept in the house and proceeded to return fire. Although this seems like a scene out of *Gunsmoke*, this probably saved the family. The return fire held the gunmen off and made them think twice about entering the house. It worked. The gunmen retreated. The family was safe. Once again it was Shelton who gave me the dreaded call. He said, "Mr. Sam, have you heard?"

I said, "No, heard what?"

"Brandon's house got shot up last night."

"I am on my way."

I got to the apartment and was dumbfounded by what I saw. Lying out in the front of Brandon's apartment were countless automatic bullet casings. The building looked like a target practice. Windows were cracked and broken with bullet holes seemingly piercing every inch of the downstairs portion of the apartment. The parking lot in front of their apartment was full of casings and broken glass. Many of the bullets that made their way inside of the apartment acted as disgruntled houseguests. Some of the bullets even exited the back walls and windows of the apartment. The bullets didn't discriminate. Many of them also went through the neighbor's wall, nearly missing a sleeping baby.

This had become the new neighborhood narrative. This horrible incident truly made Brandon's dad's words ring true. We were making a difference, but Brandon's family had a history of issues. There were five children in the family. Four of them had criminal records. Brandon was the only exception. One of his older brothers was killed by the police. During a traffic stop this brother, who was a passenger in the car, got nervous since he had a warrant hanging over his head and jumped out of the car and began the run. He ran down an alley and tried to hop a locked fence, but was tasered while on top of the fence. His body went limp and he fell off the fence onto his head and broke his neck. He died instantly. One of Brandon's nephews was murdered in the East Atlanta streets. He also has a nephew serving a life sentence with no chance of parole for murdering a known acquaintance. Life was not easy in the Bradley household.

This moment of honesty hit me hard. I said to myself that God works through all of us. He delivers us messages in the strangest of ways. You definitely can't judge the messenger. You don't have to wear Burberry or Polo to bring a message.

I actually thanked Terry Robinson, Brandon's dad, for the kind words. Anytime that you work with children, you are always very appreciative when people appreciate you. I often comment that the most underappreciated folks are persons who work in any profession that deals with children. Children are supposedly the world's greatest resource, yet oftentimes the people teaching, molding, and training them are highly underpaid and grossly overworked. It would truly be called a thankless profession if your check statement could talk.

This conversation only cemented my hopes and plans for what I had already pondered was possible. I knew that these boys were going to make it. I had been asking God for signs. It is very difficult trying to reform a child's thought process—or anyone's, for that matter. This process often contradicts the very thought of what kids and people are taught. Exhibiting the proper dress, treating people fairly, loving thy neighbor, opening doors for folks, respect for self and others, and a proper education truly make the world go 'round. When you deal with some children, you would swear that they haven't been taught anything, but the world also needs to realize that one's zip code doesn't define their plight or opportunities.

These kids persevered through a lot. They experienced incredible highs and monumental lows. But after defeating some of their circumstances, I knew they were going to be successful.

Brandon was an exceptional student and person, but all of the influences around him pointed to failure. The assault on his apartment (for which no one was ever charged) forced Brandon and his family to move out of the Villages of East Lake and into the Thomasville Heights housing project. Thomasville Heights, the concrete jungle, was also one of the worst areas in Atlanta. The neighborhood had only one entrance and one exit and they were one in the same. It's crazy that some folks are never able to get off of that merry-go-round of tough times. Thomasville Heights was located 200 yards from the U.S. Federal Penitentiary and less than 15 minutes from the Fulton County Jail.

Brandon's mother, siblings, and extended family worked in unison to protect Brandon from his environment—and he made it. Brandon would go to college on a golf scholarship. He double majored in math and accounting. He was a mainstay on the Dean's List. He was halfway into his last semester of college and about to graduate when his mother got extremely ill. Against her best wishes, he dropped out of college and went back to Atlanta to care for her. This was yet another setback, but he was determined to keep running this race. He eventually got a job working for a large corporation and worked his way up into middle management. He got married and had a few kids and eventually finished his college degree. He is very responsible with his money and he has leaned on making very sound decisions. He is doing really well and is a wonderful father.

CHAPTER 10

Elevation

"For you are my hope, O Lord God;
You are my trust from my youth."

(Psalm 71:5)

For many agonizing months, I tossed around a surplus of ideas on how to make East Lake realize that the program could be a lot more than an after-school program. The reason I had accepted the East Lake job was that I believed I could help develop a national model. I had played collegiate golf, taught school, run junior clinics, and worked for the Lincoln Heritage Council Boy Scouts of America in Louisville, Kentucky, but I saw the East Lake position as the true way to positively impact the lives of more kids.

I had created a national junior golf tournament at East Lake. I was able to handpick from the most qualified participants. With the help of one of our best volunteers in the world, Valerie Levy, I was able to select 50 great juniors for two consecutive years. I had accomplished what the national First Tee was trying to develop.

My personal goal was to mix the races and prove to the "golf world" that there were capable and qualified black golfers who could play the game at a high level.

The National Golf Foundation estimated that there are 12.5 million adult "core" golfers in the United States. They also estimated that there are 2.5 million junior golfers ages 12 to 17. Fewer than a dozen golfers of African descent play major collegiate golf. According to an NGF study in 2013, there were 1.3 million African American golfers at least 18 years of age and older. Now with the First Tee boasting figures totaling more than five million children exposed to the game of golf, I think the paltry number of blacks or blacks mixed with other races is ridiculous.

In those days, young people like Harold Villere, Joshua Wooding, Steve Hogan, Jr., Spencer Witherspoon, Brent Witcher, and Erica Battle had come to ELGC, simply to name a few, to compete. Joshua Wooding, who ended up having a stellar career at the University of Southern California, won the first East Lake tournament on the boys' side. He was only 14 years old. His even-par 72 from the tips was good enough to give him the victory.

Erica Battle, a great player at the University of South Carolina, won on the female side.

I laughed at the process because in the end my experiment worked. Many of the kids they beat, like Brent Witcher, went on to have stellar junior careers and good professional careers.

I was able to do this for two years before East Lake put the clamps on the event. There was honestly no sound reason to end the event, but nevertheless, they stopped it. It wasn't financial because Mrs. Levy and a couple of her associates had offered to pay for the event. But all of this prompted me to become very creative and it forced me to truly come up with some different ways to expose those who many never wanted to be exposed. It finally made me act.

At this point, Shelton, Willie, Brandon, and Rod were not good enough to play with these kids, but they were getting close. The four boys could shoot in the 80s, but I began to notice that the technological explosion in golf was changing the game. All of the equipment that I gave the children in the golf academy had been donated, basically hand-me-downs. The balls we used had been donated. They were balls picked out of area lakes.

I had already been placing these children in tournaments and the discrepancy was huge. The other kids were out-driving us and making their balls spin on the green. Our balls seemed to be made out of rock, only they had soft white covers. Imagine Michael Jordan crossing over on a defender with holes in an old pair of Chuck Taylor sneakers and the defender is sporting a new pair of Lebron's.

This analogy is accurate with golf equipment. I had the head of the foundation and others in key positions ask me why they should spend a lot of money on equipment. They said good golfers should be able to hit anything. These comments were insane.

One day on the way to work, I decided to push the envelope. I took a step that honestly could have backfired on me. I took a step that could have forced me and my wife to put on boxing gloves in order to rectify the damages. On the way to work, I stopped by an Edwin Watts golf store out on Pleasant Hill Road in Gwinnett County and I bought $3,000 worth of golf equipment. This was essentially about eight sets of golf clubs. I bought sets of Titleist and TaylorMade. I purchased only the irons. I didn't think of buying the woods. This would have dug a deeper hole in my pocket.

After dropping the clubs off at the course, I went and filled out an expense slip in order to get reimbursed. I then went about my natural day awaiting the inevitable confrontation.

Working at the East Lake Community Foundation, expenses and reimbursements were huge. The accountant went over the financials with a fine-tooth comb. I honestly thought some of it was racially motivated, but it never bothered me. I actually really liked all of my coworkers. They truly cared and respected the mission of the foundation.

Think about this scenario: How many black chief financial officers are working for the top 200 companies in the United States? For this matter, how many of these top companies are headed by blacks? Point made! I was raised right. If I didn't learn anything else at Carver High, it was how to count and execute advanced math. I would never steal funds or fudge the numbers. I believed in karma. I believed that you get out of something what you put into it. The accountant asked me a million questions. The head of the foundation seemed to be a little perturbed, but he never quite got around to tripping about it. I think he had bigger fish to fry.

East Lake repaid me for my expenses and no one in my office ever mentioned it. But strangely enough, Walter Ashmore, who was president of East Lake Golf Club, called me and wanted to talk. The conversation changed everything. He said, "Sam, I noticed a rather large reimbursement that we recently paid you." He said in order to cut costs, next time ask him or Rick Burton, director of golf, for some help. He said we could get anything either free or at a reduced cost. I thought the conversation was on point and it really inspired me to continue to do what I was doing. All was cool. Mr. Ashmore was an old white man. I respected him because he was about business, and I knew there were not a lot of "us" in his initial upbringings.

Mr. Ashmore and Charlie were about the same age. One day Charlie told me it wasn't until he joined the Army that he realized how important and intelligent black people were. He said he was impressed by his sergeant in the Army and it totally changed his outlook. Growing up the only blacks he knew worked for his family. They served his family. They were his butlers and maids. He said his sergeant in the Army was the first black person he had ever met in an authoritative position. He said he really liked his sergeant and it changed his entire view of the world. This is why I loved Charlie. He was transparent and truthful. Walter Ashmore's comments were graciously accepted.

I quietly laughed and said, "Yes, sir." Walter might have known, maybe he didn't. But I had been trying to go through the professional staff at East Lake for everything from clothing to expenses. I hadn't found anyone outside of Janie Stratigos, who seemed to understand the struggle. It didn't matter anymore now because I knew this would never be an issue again. When I accepted the job, I vowed that one day my golfers would stand on the tee box and the only difference between them and everyone else would be the melanin of their skin. I can say I stayed long enough to see this come to fruition. I worked very diligently to create relationships with clothing and equipment manufactures. We also placed a couple of clothing executives on our large foundation board. We totally cut our costs in half. We also got a lot for free. Shirts, pants, shorts, socks, clubs, travel arrangements, flights, shoes, rain suits, balls, gloves, and anything golf related became a normal occurrence.

CHAPTER 11

Locked Up

"Blessed are ye, when men shall revile you, and
persecute you, and shall say all manner of
evil against you falsely, for my sake."

(Matthew 5:11)

On a beautiful September day after a Stanford University golf practice, I received a call around 3 p.m. Pacific Time. It was Shelton back in the ATL. His voice was elevated and he was frantic. I had come to know all of the boys' voice fluctuations and typical idiosyncrasies. These were my kids. I knew them like the back of my hand.

His tone on the phone was enough to scare me because Shelton was normally one of the happiest young men in the world. My parents loved him. He was always smiling, but this time the fluctuation in his voice was different.

I spent the beginning of the conversation trying to get him to calm down in an effort to understand his Atlanta (Dirty South) accent. He kept reiterating "these folks are trippin'." He said, "Mr. Sam, they are trippin'. Brandon and Willie are in jail." The word "jail" typically had different connotations for me and the boys. Part of it was because of the rap music they listened to and part of it was their upbringing. The boys always joked about not getting arrested and locked up. Because they had so many friends and relatives behind bars, their ghetto definition of jail differed. Jail had been a revolving door for many of the residents. The children in the neighborhood saw people come and go to lockup. We had taken field trips to the jail trying to utilize the city of Atlanta's Scared Straight program, but we stopped visiting when I realized that no one was afraid. Some of the kids looked forward to the visits. We would walk through the jail and inmates would call my students by name and dap them up during the visit. This is when the visits ended.

Before I responded I looked at my phone and saw several missed calls from Tammy Brown, Willie's mother. I hadn't been able to respond to her calls because I had been at golf practice all day. I had told myself I would call her during one of my afternoon breaks. I honestly forgot to call her. I had left the dirty-dirty and moved out west to serve as an assistant coach at Stanford University. I was the first black assistant golf coach in the Pac-10 Conference (now the Pac-12). I eventually became the first and only black head men's golf coach in the history of a BCS school. Stanford was an incredible institution. The home of champions, the home of one names: Watson, Notah, Casey, and Tiger. The only university that can boast three alumni who have been presidents of the United States Golf Association.

I was now three hours behind the boys in time and I was now a "true" phone call away. After Shelton and I began the conversation, his words started to sink in. Willie and Brandon are in jail. My first thoughts were simple and selfish. Why now? It must be a mistake. They are funny and crazy kids, but they are not stupid. I asked Shelton the one basic and simple question. What happened? After hearing his response, I knew Shelton was serious. Although he was always smiling, laughing, and joking, I knew this was different. He respects me and he has always been honest with me. I heard something in his voice that I hadn't heard from him since his mom had locked him out of the house for not getting up and cleaning the house at 6 a.m. on a Sunday morning.

Shelton was serious and he was totally disturbed, bothered, angry, and confused. He said, "Willie and Brandon had been accused of robbing a guy on their home golf course, the Charlie Yates Golf Course."

When I heard this, I again replied, "This must be a mistake," but this crap was real. I was actually thinking this was some bullshit. These guys were a lot of things, but criminals they were not. Shelton and Rod had explained the entire scenario to me. They filled in all of the details and pinpointed why they thought what they thought. These fellows were very intelligent and very transparent. They were also honest and authentic.

According to the boys' account, the Atlanta police had come to the Charlie Yates Golf Course with the intent and sole purpose of arresting Brandon and Willie. The eight cops looked like two foursomes having a really bad round of golf. They weren't smiling and they almost looked as if they enjoyed it. The head pro had come out to witness the spectacle. They walked up on the green dressed in duty blue uniforms and stood like a strong pre-shot routine.

The big burly cop immediately walked over to Brandon. His wiry, testosterone-laced sidekicks cornered Willie. They read both boys their Miranda rights. They were both snatched and arrested. The officers grabbed the boys and placed their arms behind their backs, cuffed them, placed them on golf carts. So much for birdies and pars; now these two needed prayers.

Like a terrible golfer playing on a major championship course from the tips, the po-po (affectionate name for the police) was very intimidating. Why did eight cops have to come to the golf course to arrest these boys? Why couldn't they allow the boys to complete the round? Why wouldn't they go through the foundation and set up a private arrest? Was this going to make the news? Were the boys going to lose their scholarships? (The boys had all been offered and signed college golf scholarships to play at Grambling University.) These questions and a million more were making their rounds through my head.

Our minds are unsuspecting prisons, capturing our pulse because it controls our thoughts. Shelton and Rod were witnessing this intrigue like a bad B movie. They were ushered into the back of the squad car and quietly driven off without much fanfare. Big question: What the hell just happened? Why did they get arrested? Here is an interesting factoid: Since the location of their high school was in the hood, all of the boys were used to the "hook" (another endearing term for the police). The "hook" was always present. When they came to get you, they came to get you. Many of their peers had gotten hemmed up (arrested) in school.

The foundation sought out Shelton because of his relationship with Brandon and Willie and they began to gather the facts in an effort to free the boys. Now in jail, Willie's prodigious swan-like swing and Brandon's incredible length off the tee meant absolutely nothing. The boys would later say that life seems truly crazy when your innate freedoms have been removed.

The neighborhood was buzzing. The word was starting to spread.

Shelton drove his clean, green Saturn that I had given him for $1 down Memorial Drive to the jail. The Dekalb County Jail was only about a 10-minute drive from the neighborhood. The jail staff allowed him an opportunity to speak with both boys. We actually knew the sheriff really well. The boys had golfed with him on several occasions. They constantly professed their innocence. The irony to Shelton was that both boys were totally oblivious to the entire situation. They honestly didn't have a clue why they had been arrested.

Willie's mother had found out that her baby was in jail and she was going nuts. Her older son had run into a few legal issues about six months earlier. He was a junior in college and thought he could make a few extra dollars by selling a little weed. He always talked about being rich. He always talked about Bill Gates. He always talked about making a difference in the world with his computer prowess. Well, he might do that one day, but the first thing he needed to do was graduate from college and make money the old-fashion way.

Brandon's mother was dumbfounded. She always told me that he was her baby and he was really going to do some big things with his life. She was really proud of him. She was definitely proud of his clean legal record. Although she couldn't explain it, she was truly proud of his math ability. Brandon was an exceptional math student. He was taking advance calculus classes and yet he never took books home. (The neighborhood didn't treat kids kindly carrying bookbags after school.) This kept him from getting ridiculed by the neighborhood. I never figured out why so many of "us" don't embrace an education. If blacks embrace their history, they would be proud to take books home. We are descendants of the creators of the alphabet, the ancient mathematicians, and the people who discovered the stars. Think about the building of the pyramids. Need I say more?

Their high school graduation was less than a month away. Both boys were charged with armed robbery. They were booked at the DeKalb County Jail. They were forced to put on the orange monkey suit.

Getting caught up in the system and developing a rap sheet was the one thing I knew could derail their golfing careers, but more importantly their lives. Their credit reports and background-check record were the one initial rite-of-passage test that they had to pass in order to even have a chance at a successful life. The other number was related to children. Statistics proved that students who were able to delay having children until at least their 25th birthday increased their chance of success.

Brandon and Willie were jailed on that Friday. Shelton told me their first opportunity to go before a judge would be on Tuesday. This was terrible! They were going to have to spend a minimum of four days behind bars for a crime, in my mind, that they could have never committed. To make matters worse, bail was set at $50,000.

I knew they weren't capable of such a terrible act. The more important question to anyone close to the East Lake family would be why. Why would they do something this asinine on their home golf course? My dad always said that you don't shit where you eat or sleep. Another puzzling point was how they could have committed such a despicable act when they were in school!

Their accuser—a local, prominent, white bank vice president at SunTrust—was salty. He said two young black guys had robbed him. He described them as dark-skinned, short, around five-foot-eight or five-nine—stocky guys with a head full of braids. Growing up we always heard that white folks think all black folks look alike. We could be as black as night or as light as a lemon, but to many of them we all looked alike.

My first question was simple. How can someone in America accuse one of us of anything and we automatically get arrested? I always thought we were innocent until proven guilty. When you are black, you are guilty until proven innocent. I only have to think back on my own personal experiences, and that's when this scenario really hit home. I have been stopped 13 times by the police and been accused of looking suspicious, asked if I was speeding, told the music was too loud (while the radio was actually off), told that I fit a specific profile, and told that I shouldn't be able to afford the vehicle that I was driving at my age. I have been asked a million times why I was driving in certain neighborhoods. They couldn't believe that I had white friends.

I guess when you are a white businessman who runs the local SunTrust Bank and you accuse two young black guys, the law reverses to your favor. The description was insane. Neither Willie nor Brandon were five-foot-eight or five-nine. This was the most glaring inconsistency. Brandon is six-four and Willie is six-three and they are both long and thin. The second inconsistency in question was the time of the incident. The supposed time of the act was troubling. Brandon and Shelton had the same fifth-period class over at Southside High School. On the day in question, Brandon was in class. Willie was also in school that morning, but he left early in order to get a haircut before the big collegiate signing with the local news station. Truthfully, they were all leaving directly after school to go get haircuts, but Willie was lazy and he didn't want to go to class anyway. Think about it! This was the opportunity of a lifetime for these boys. Getting their hair cut was a really big deal to them and their families. The East Lake Community Foundation was a marketing machine. Your appearance played an integral role in their marketing perception.

The accuser said that he was robbed on April 28, 2006 (this just so happened to be my son's birthday) at 2 p.m. on the 17th hole of the Charlie Yates Golf Course. The National Letter of Intent was afforded to you in order to play collegiate athletics. The boys had a scheduled appointment with Fox News at 4 p.m. The boys would be on the range hitting balls before meeting with Fox News.

Nevertheless, the boys sat in jail for four days hoping for a miracle. Tammy Brown and Mary Bradley, Brandon's mother, didn't have the money for the bail. How could they afford bail? Why should they have to afford bail? The descriptions didn't match. Everything was hearsay. It was one man's word against two boys' word.

I always preached to the boys that it's okay to dream because miracles do happen. Look at the situation! These boys were getting ready to go to college.

Early that Tuesday morning, the boys went before the judge. As they approached the bench, they noticed their audience. They began to quietly sob. Tom Cousins, his daughter, and her family and their representatives from the foundation sat in attendance. The boys were being represented by one of the best big-money attorneys in Atlanta. Tom Cousins has not only placed his beliefs in the boys' innocence, but also his financial backing. The boys were released on bail, but their case was still going to happen. This dream had turned into an instant nightmare. This was a travesty. This story of injustice is still happening and it still has our blood boiling.

CHAPTER 12
Statistics

"'For I know the plans I have for you,' declares the LORD,
'plans to prosper you and not to harm you, plans to
give you hope and a future.'"

(Jeremiah 29:11)

For the entire duration of my nine-year tenure at East Lake, the powers to be had always relied on crime statistics to prove a point. The crime statistics indeed proved a major point. These numbers lamented the point that "change was a-coming." These statistics were the defining element that the neighborhood had changed or been reborn if you will. The criminal statistics were indeed gold. These numbers would also highlight that increased property values weren't far behind. Think about it! In the beginning of 1998, you could buy an old dilapidated house in the neighborhood for $35,000 to $50,000. In January of 2006, the same dilapidated house had increased in value to at least $250,000. The house I am describing is an empty, old, crack-infested house. A new house in the neighborhood today in 2017 will start at a minimum of $700,000.

The numbers were also important to the PGA Tour. In 1998, the PGA Tour held the first of what is now an indefinite amount of PGA Tour Championships at East Lake Golf Club. This has transitioned into the finale of the Tour Fed Ex Cup. The Tour prides itself in advertising their generosity to local charities and neighborhoods. This tournament was kicking off more than $600,000 annually to the East Lake Foundation. A huge percentage went to the foundation and the rest went to their First Tee endeavor.

The statistics were also vital to the total restoration of the project. The initial goal was to search the United States and recruit 100 top Fortune 500 firms to become corporate members. Before Mr. Cousins purchased the club, he offered the current resident members an opportunity to join the club at the ridiculously low rate of $25,000. This number is amazing. The going rate for local memberships in Atlanta was around $55,000. The cost of private memberships out here in California is two to three times that amount. The crux of the membership declined the offer. This was a huge mistake. They didn't realize that Mr. Cousins didn't do anything without proper planning and execution. They also didn't realize that he felt that God was leading him to make these changes. God doesn't make mistakes.

Everyone knew that no corporate monster would join the club if there was a chance that they might get robbed or "jacked" on the course or on the adjacent streets heading to the course. The crackheads, the junkies, the major drug trade was all gone in the blink of an eye. The Atlanta Police Department literally changed the local scene overnight. This was amazing considering the place that was previously known as "Little Vietnam" was now markedly better. The police had been known to ignore calls in this area affectionately known as Zone 6. The threat of getting jacked up at the light near Pops, the Korean man's store, automatically disappeared.

The arrest of the boys and the subsequent media blitz could have crushed all of the positive and wonderful feel-good stories in one instant. But it didn't! The incident never made the paper.

The story disappeared. It never made even a quick blurb on the news. I was glad that it didn't come out because it could have also jeopardized the golf scholarships for the boys.

Willie said, "It was mistaken identity. I think about it all the time. It taught me to do right. It could have ruined my life. It is dirty that people can accuse you of something and you didn't do it. People are in jail and they are innocent. I am trying to keep my nose clean. I don't have time to take any negative risks. All of my college dreams could have disappeared. God has opened up a lot of doors. I am going to be successful. I have graduated from college now. Golf got me this far. I am not going to mess anything up."

The attorney, along with the local district attorney, approached the accuser, explaining the situation. The accuser was confronted with a big-time defense team and a slew of bad publicity if indeed his accusations were found to be untrue. The accuser had made a major mistake. The site of seeing Mr. Cousins in the courtroom rocked the room. In the television sitcoms, criminals were afraid of Lee Majors, the $6 million man. In real life, false accusers and their attorneys had to fear that the real $900 million man would strike back. He had helped build most of Atlanta and he had worked too hard to allow over-the-top racism and racial profiling to affect his creation.

After a couple of months of absolutely nothing, the charges were dropped. The boys were able to relax and resume their normal life.

Brandon said, "I felt like I was doing something good as a black man and folks were trying to take it away. I was trying not to think about jail. I didn't deserve the poor treatment. Before the arrest, I knew I was going to get a chance to make a difference. I knew that once I finished college, I wouldn't have to live check to check. I was ready to get out of jail and follow my dreams."

The incident was troubling, regardless of the outcome. The neighborhood found out the real deal. The guy did indeed get robbed. The real "perps" were also black with "twists." The major difference was their weight and their height. The real criminals were a lot shorter than Willie and Brandon and a lot heavier.

I guess the accuser wasn't taught along with the rest of us that all blacks don't look alike. Too bad! The one point that didn't escape me was money. If Mr. Cousins and the foundation, regardless of their reasons, hadn't come to the aid of these boys, they could potentially still be locked up today. Where were they going to get bail money? They wouldn't have had a quick and speedy trial. They would not have graduated high school. They would have lost their golf scholarships. Would the district attorney and local detectives have been as interested in getting to the bottom of the case? The boys would have probably become statistics.

More than 50 percent of young black men in Atlanta don't graduate high school. I know Mr. Cousins and the foundation had wonderfully positive motives and truly believed in these boys. According to a recent report, there is an estimated 10 percent of the prison population that is indeed innocent. Many have suggested that this number is actually far higher. When the percentage is broken down according to race, the estimated number rises even more.

But there were also a couple of other troubling issues with the entire ordeal. A couple of the professionals at Charlie Yates Golf Course treated the boys as if they were guilty first and innocent later. The boys weren't allowed to come to the golf course to practice or play. This was tough because they needed to practice to get ready for summer tournaments. This was also troubling because the golf course had served as a safe haven for the kids for the past seven years. This incident also exposed others. It showed all of us that there were people in their immediate circle who didn't have their best interest at heart. It taught them that being a young black man in America would come with some bumps and bruises. To some, whether we are five-eight or six-four we are essentially guilty first. None of the descriptions matched—tone of skin color, height, weight— but we are black.

CHAPTER 13
Shelton

"Love does not delight in evil but rejoices with the truth.
It always protects, always trusts, always hopes,
always perseveres."
(1 Corinthians 13:6-7)

For Shelton, golf had become a natural family affair. Shelton was the second child of Pam Davis. He had developed into a very good golfer. He was a jovial-natured young man and he had one of the best inner spirits in the world. He was nicer than my son. Imagine a smiling young Mike Tyson minus the slurring of his words hitting balls on the range. This was Shelton…and yes the analogy was fitting. Years later I watched him literally knock Carl Williams out at the golf clubhouse. A shot to the jaw and Carl's eyes flickered like an old light bulb. He had asked Carl to stop poking him and getting in his face talking trash, but he wouldn't. Shelton snapped! The vision of the movie *Friday* was evident. We all stood over Carl hoping that he wasn't seriously hurt.

Shelton's older sister, Yas'man, was one of the best if not my best golfer in the program. She always befuddled me. She smiled a bunch, but damn she always sucked her thumb. She had grown to five-eight and was built like a young woman, but still sucked her thumb. I always thought it was symptomatic of delayed development of some sort. I am no therapist, but there had to be a deeper meaning. She was a brilliant young lady.

She had developed a great golf resume. Yas had won a bunch of the junior events and she was probably better than all of the boys. As a ninth-grader, she had been told by several collegiate coaches that she would definitely receive a full scholarship upon graduation from high school.

But the strangest thing happened. She didn't graduate. In the ninth grade, she was an honor student. Her grade point average was north of 3.6, but she lost the desire to complete what she had started. She didn't finish school. She fell victim to the streets. When listening to the Ying Yang Twins (a local rap group from the ATL that also went to Crim High School, the same high school as Yas, they rapped about "All Zones"; all of the madness was highlighted). The city of Atlanta was divided into zones. The East Lake area was Zone 6. This area had become very popular in rap lyrics for being tough, crime-ridden, and very raggedy. Actually, Crim High School has produced a few famous folks: Inky Johnson (motivational speaker), James Davis (football), Ying Yang Twins (rap music), Richard Dent (football), and Mo Lewis (played at Murphy High, which became Crim).

During one of my occasional trips to the school to secretly check up on her, I passed her walking down Memorial Drive. I was thinking why in the hell is she walking down the street at this time of day? I did an immediate U-turn, picked her up, and called her mother. She asked me for a ride to her house because she insisted that she had some female issues. Me being pretty oblivious to female issues, I took her at her word for being out of school and dropped her off. But something didn't feel right. Since her high school was only a mile away, I finished what I had set out to do and paid the school a visit. I had a great relationship with the administrators and the teachers. They would give me any and all of the pertinent information about all of my East Lake children. I think they were so excited to have someone on the outside who cared that they would have done anything I asked them to do.

I first met with the registrar and everything seemed cool. This was always my first stop. This was the quickest and easiest way to check. The attendance lists were always great, or at least I thought so. But this time I did something a little different that would inconvenience her teachers and take a little more time, but it would give me more information when I talked to her mother. Whenever I went by the schools and dealt with the children, I always gave the parents a visit or a phone call. I visited those who didn't have telephones and called those who did.

I checked with her first, second, and third period teachers and everything seemed cool. After checking with the fourth through sixth period teachers I found myself in a panic. Yas had been showing up for her first few classes. The third period teacher takes the attendance and then submits it to the attendance office. Yas had missed 67 consecutive days from her fourth through sixth period classes. The teachers were as dumbfounded as me. They said they had honestly not seen her enough to know what was going on in her life. I confronted her and quickly surmised that the quest to get high (smoke weed) and have sex outweighed the scientific periodic tables and anything else they were learning in school.

As a result, Yas dropped out of school in the 10th grade. Her dream of playing collegiate golf had just dropped down the tubes and her dream was deferred. This was also very unfortunate for Shelton because he looked up to her and they were very close. He was experiencing the residual firsthand.

Shelton dared to be different. He did his best in school and he also got a job. Shelton was working at the golf course on the weekends. He was sharing his check with his mother. He also paid the only bill that he had, which was a cell phone bill. Things were really looking up until one fateful morning.

One Sunday morning around six o'clock, Shelton received a call from his mom. His mother had sacrificed a lot of her personal wants and dreams early on for Shelton and his two other siblings. She had placed all of her personal interests, which included relationships, vacations, etc., on hold to see that the kids were getting where they needed to go and what they needed as it related to golf. On this particular morning, everything went nuts. Pam called from her fiancé Billy's house. It was early, but she wanted Shelton to get up on Sunday morning and clean the apartment before he went to work at the golf course. Shelton said, "Yes, ma'am," but he unintentionally went back to sleep. I will also state for the record that Shelton was one of the most responsible young men I knew. He was always neatly groomed and on time, and he would do exactly what you asked him to do. He was always courteous and kind. All of these qualities were about to be tested over the course of the next 12 months.

Shelton was now a 10th-grader. He was beginning to focus on college. His job at the golf course was enabling him to help pay bills and save a few dollars and it allowed him to work on his game. Shelton woke up a few hours later. He began cleaning the house. He had cleaned nearly all of it, but realized that time was running short and he had to go to work. He quickly showered and ran around the corner to the golf course. His first order of business at the course on this beautiful Sunday morning was to pick range balls. He gathered his old, beat-up golf shoes and jumped in the range picker.

While picking balls on the range, he received a call from his mother. She asked the question that changed it all. "Shelton, did you finish cleaning the house?" His response, which was honest, was, "I cleaned most of it, but I will finish the rest when I get off work." His mother blew a gasket. She exploded! She ordered Shelton to return home and place his cell phone in her room. To a lot of folks, revoking cell phone privileges doesn't mean much, but to Shelton it meant everything.

Shelton's issues were simple. First, Shelton had bought the cell phone and he paid the bill. Secondly, there were certain times when he wasn't allowed to use the house phone. Lastly, in his mind, who was it going to kill that a little cleaning was left undone on a Sunday morning, especially since his mother had spent the night with her fiancé anyway? This was my thought because I had three kids and they often needed a slight nudge or subtle threat to clean my house. My kids fought and sassed when I asked them to pick up their clothes, let alone clean the house.

The bottom line was simple. Whether Shelton was wrong or right, respectful or disrespectful, he disobeyed his mother's wishes and refused to give her his cell phone.

When she returned home, the war started. She gave him another opportunity to rectify his disobedience, which was to place his phone in her room, but he again refused. She felt hurt. She felt as if his act of defiance would only worsen. As my mom use to say, she thought he was trying to act grown. She in turn told Shelton that he had to leave her house. Shelton was hurt, but he obliged and packed a bag and left. "I was crushed that I had to leave home. I loved my mom and I know she loved me, but I thought I was doing the right thing," Shelton said.

This was an egregious mistake by his mother, at least in my eyes. Shelton was doing well in school, plus at the end of the day he didn't have anywhere else to go. His dad had never been in the picture and several of his relatives had incurred run-ins with the law. He called his dad's mother. She was old but nice. Grandma opened her house to him.

But there was one catch; her house was out of control. Grandma's house was probably the worst alternative. It was a small house located in Southwest Atlanta. We all referred to the area as the SWATS. Grandma had also allowed Shelton's sister Yas'man to live there. Yas had also experienced a run-in with her mother a year earlier and had sought refuge, but for the wrong reasons. Grandma also had a hodgepodge of six or seven additional deviants living there, most of whom had checkered criminal pasts. The house was dark and smoky and it was located 10 yards from the drug corner. Bathroom windows were always cracked so that the weed smoke could quietly escape. Hoopties and other ghetto fabulous cars draped the driveway and the neighboring side streets. In this part of town everyone rode dirty. Drug selling was a given and the neighborhood norm, and it was running rampant on Grandma's street.

The house had been raided twice by the Drug Enforcement Agency (DEA), but they didn't scare anyone. They simply repaired the broken glass and redecorated and commenced to doing what they did best, which was hustle. The stench of weed and alcohol totally permeated the fabric. The house appeared to be a ridiculous refuge to a lot of folks who simply didn't want to work and loved to get high, but more importantly do absolutely nothing. But the grandmother was very accommodating. She gave Shelton a place to sleep on the couch. She also told Shelton to stay away from the corners and she told his cousins to make sure the dope boys stayed away from him. It was amazing. She essentially tried to create a ghetto circle of protection around him.

Shelton initially tried to act as if he wasn't bothered by the eviction and he was putting up the perception that he didn't miss a beat, but I knew better. Shelton couldn't fool me. The other kids in the program couldn't fool me. They were like my children with the exception that I couldn't write them off on my taxes. I knew him and them, but I could see that he was hurting. I started buying him a monthly MARTA card. This card allowed him to use the bus or the train from anywhere in the city that utilized public transportation. I also noticed that he was now always hungry.

Shelton was a big boy and he loved to eat. At five-eight and about 220 pounds, something had to quench his appetite. I also noticed that his performance in school started to dip. He began spending more and more time at his girlfriend's house. I think he might have just experienced his first taste of "honey." I honestly thought he was going over to see his lady and leaving at night, but I soon realized that he was eating all of his meals and spending the night over there as well. This insanity went on for a while until it bothered me. I had to figure out an alternative. This entire set-up with the girlfriend wreaked.

I sought some help. I went to one of my closest friends, Sheldon Holloway. Holloway was in the process of buying a new five-bedroom house. He had also recently been blessed with a wonderful baby boy. I asked Sheldon the question. "Can Shelton come to live with you and your family?" Sheldon said he thought it was a great idea, but he had to check with his wife. His wonderful wife said, "Yes." She was actually pretty stern, but fair. Sheldon instantly commissioned his Uncle Carl, who like him was from Liberty City in Miami, to come up to the ATL and fix one of the rooms specifically for Shelton. Sheldon even bought Shelton some furniture that he liked.

This was a great storybook ending, right? Wrong. The experiment didn't last.

Shelton seemed very resistant to what I thought was a normal life. Funny how our experiences carve out our realities and expectations. Sheldon was a lot like me. We had both been raised by a mother and father. We had both been products of a lot of household rules. He and his brother had played sports in college. His neighborhood was a thousand times rougher than mine, but we were like brothers. My brother and I had played sports in college. Family was incredibly important to both of us. He loved his job in the neighborhood and he loved kids.

When I first met him, he worked at the YMCA. He was always searching for ways to reach more kids. He was very spiritual and very "real" with the kids and their families. This eventually led to an opportunity as a physical education instructor at the new school in the neighborhood. He was also a new golfer. He came to me one day and asked for some help. I told him that if he volunteered on a regular basis, I would allow him to play for free at the course. I also told him that by the simple process of being around the driving range, which would become his ghetto osmosis, he would become a better golfer. If he were actually trying to help teach our beginning juniors the basics of the game, the evolution would work.

Sheldon's game was improving and he was out volunteering every day after school. His presence was similar to having another instructor on staff. This is where the difference with Shelton became evident. Without even realizing the simple dynamics, Shelton was used to dysfunction. Although his mother believed in structure, their lives weren't very structured. Sheldon asked him to do his homework in a certain area of the house. He asked him to be home by a certain time. He asked him to clean. I thought these were all normal requests, but it was difficult for Shelton to adjust.

The living arrangement with Sheldon slowly deteriorated. I figured something had to be done. Months had now elapsed and the light at the end of the tunnel was becoming very dim. I took Shelton over to his girlfriend's house one day for dinner. I knew that I wouldn't get many more opportunities to do something to improve the situation. Instead of leaving when I dropped him off, I parked and went in. Months later, Shelton joked that his girlfriend's mother thought I was cute. She was happy that I came in. I laughed with him, but nevertheless, I think the tide started to turn. I expressed my concerns to the girlfriend's mother and strangely enough she was on my side. She agreed! I also didn't let it slip that I had spoken with Shelton's mother Pam for the umpteenth time. To my surprise, she said that she would allow him to come back to live at home, but he was still going to have to abide by her rules. I was amazed that the refusal of a cell phone could create a situation like this but it did. Shelton said, "I hated it. It was messed up. I love my mom. How was she going to kick her own son out and I hadn't done anything wrong? No one is going to be there for me all the time. It was a great lesson learned. I still love her, though."

Shelton and I left after dinner and I explained the scenario to him. We packed his shit and bounced. I reiterated my thoughts and feelings. He agreed and I took him and all of his things to his mother's house. I honestly felt as though we lost an important golf year in our quest to prepare him for college. That year could have sealed his fate, but it didn't. Shelton went home and he has never looked back. He has carved out a very successful life for himself. He is now a golf instructor in Atlanta, giving back to the community.

CHAPTER 14

SAT Test

"Teach me knowledge and good judgment,
for I trust your commands."

(Psalm 119:66)

Rod, Eric, Shelton, Willie, and Brandon had improved their golf games and their academic standings in school. They were developing into wonderful young men.

College was within their grasp. I signed the boys up to take the SAT test. I figured that the first test would give me an indicator about their academic test-taking ability along with showing me where they stood in regards to being eligible to play collegiate golf.

The NCAA mandates that all student-athletes have to maintain at least a 2.0 grade point average and score at least an 850 on the SAT. These figures actually fluctuate on the NCAA sliding scale. The lower the grade point average, the higher the SAT test scores need to be. The GPA is also based on the actual core classes. This meant that we had to throw out all of the gym classes, art classes, and weight-lifting classes.

The scores came back. I had asked each boy after the test how they had done. They all felt pretty good. The general consensus was that the test was simple, or at least this is what I thought I heard. ("Mr. Sam, the test was easy.") They guessed at a lot of the answers because they didn't know a lot of the material, but all in all, they thought they had probably reached a qualifying score. The scores came back and they were low. WTF! They were ridiculously low. They were like dayyyyuuuuummmmm low. They didn't qualify on their first try.

I knew now that we were in for the battle of our lives. Two of the boys scored in the high 600s and four boys in the low 700s. I had signed up a couple additional neighborhood kids. Eric Davis, who was Shelton's brother, and Tony Clark. Tony was also a neighborhood kid. He was getting recruited to play football. I never really figured out where his football prowess came from because I couldn't even remember him playing Pop Warner. He was fast; he could really run. I have no idea where it came from, but he was crazy talented.

This was the one moment that I really wasn't prepared to face. The standardized testing conundrum had aroused the country. Many thought the test was culturally biased and meritless, whereas some felt as if it were the only true academic barometer to gauge the real performance of students. I have always thought that the test was biased. I never understood how one test could determine your career path. Everyone is not a great test taker. We are also products of our academic environments. If we are not raised in great schools, then securing the knowledge to ace these tests would be virtually impossible. It was scary to think that a test could determine your future. I still don't believe that one test should have this type of power over your life.

I had been prepared to help them improve their golfing ability. I knew the golf swing. I am a student of the game. I was also prepared to help improve their social skills. I had been through a bevy of etiquette trainings as a kid and a young adult. I had learned from the best. The table manners, the napkins on lap, looking in eyes when shaking hands, the "yes, ma'ams" and the "no, ma'ams," the art of dressing, what colors match, how the shirts and ties are supposed to hang, what clothes apply during which season, how to set tables, how to balance checkbooks, and how to manage your money. I had gotten the boys bank accounts at SunTrust. I had worked with the boys on making reservations. They had frequent flyer numbers and they had learned how to pack for short and long trips. We had worked on personal grooming—importance of shaving, haircuts, perceptions from the rest of the world.

The boys were great. It hadn't always been without some questions or reluctance, but in the end, this group of boys followed suit. Willie and Rod had gold grills in their mouths. I teased them because they wanted to be hip, cool, and fake "ballers," but I also teased them because they had bought the grills at the flea market on the low-low. I told them to get a good dental plan because the fake grills would probably ruin their gums. I had also battled all of them about their choice of hairstyle. The styles ranged from twists to braids to afros to dreads. I can even remember the time Willie showed up at the course with a perm. Willie was really "superfly" with a golf bag.

What very conservative businessman is going to hire these boys with the want-to-be Ziggy Marley look on their head? What very conservative businesswoman is going to hire them with the big, baggy clothes and the gold grills in their mouths? Although getting their undergraduate degrees in whatever would be a start, their golfing ability would eventually serve as their Ph.D in life. But none of this would mean anything if they were to shoot themselves in the foot because of something they could control. I preached to them to at least get a foot in the door before you go nuts. Learn how to play the game of life.

All of this seemed so surreal now since we had just gotten their test scores back. Life is funny. Life allows some of us to realize or rationalize the obstacles, and it enables some of us to rise to the challenge. Some of us give positive lip service to the challenge, but innately some of us are terrified and initially don't even think positive outcomes are possible. Life also seems to stop some of us cold turkey. People are too paralyzed to try. People quit! The self-esteem and the personal self-defeatism mindset is oftentimes too great a challenge to overcome for a lot of people. This group embraced the challenges and rolled up their sleeves in an effort to create change.

All of these boys outwardly said they were willing to rise to the challenge. They would do whatever it took in order to make it to college.

I believed the lip service, but I also realized quickly that the boys didn't know what they were up against. This was the chimera or neighborhood Deebo that everyone feared.

This SAT issue was befuddling. I had been a really good student. I was very good with numbers, but English was definitely my strength. I knew that I could help them with the verbal part of this, but this was a lot deeper. This was a systemic failure. Atlanta Public Schools were deplorable. I am surprised no one has sued APS for neglect. The school system has endured so many academic scandals. The truth and belief in the APS landscape was very low.

These guys also didn't have time for someone to reteach 10.5 years of educational material that had seemingly been ignored. If I were being honest with myself, I would imagine that it wouldn't have to be retaught. APS had turned its back on these youth. Most of this material was probably never taught.

The situation was in dire straits. The greatest part about this entire stressful situation was the boys. They were totally oblivious to all of it. They felt a little stress, but they also didn't know what they didn't know. This element of youthful exuberance is great. The other beauty in the situation was that none of their friends had done great on the SAT. It is amazing what the power of mediocrity does. None of their teachers had inquired into their SAT test-taking abilities. I had to initially go through a million hoops to simply get SAT vouchers for the boys to take the test. They couldn't afford to pay to take the test. The government gives Title I schools the ability to pay for needy kids to take the SAT.

The principal at Southside High School was an amazing lady. She was great. The situation made me ponder the possibilities. Did poor children even know that there were vouchers available? Did other kids in the school know that they offered a free SAT class? How many students had ever visited their guidance counselors? Did the guidance counselors see most of these students as lost causes? Were people working there every day simply trying to collect a paycheck? How many colleges were visiting the high school for academics instead of sports? Was it cool to go to college? I learned that some of the schools in Decatur and Atlanta offered in-school day care services for the babies of the students. Please go figure!

I maintained a great connection with the athletic director at Southside, Guy Harris, who also doubled as a teacher for a couple of the boys. Guy was always there when I needed report cards, teacher's schedules, and also frequent updates. He was always helpful.

But even with his help, he couldn't get the boys to the promised land by himself. I went over to Southside and met with the principal, Dr. Carter. She took her time to meet with me and she promised all of the school services to help the boys achieve their goals. Although she was great, it hadn't occurred to everyone who worked in the building that we were there to help these kids go to college.

I struggled to get the registrar to come on board, but it eventually happened. I also bugged about six teachers to death until they started staying in constant contact with me.

The school also notified me that they offered an SAT class, but these boys weren't in it. The guys hadn't known the class existed.

I needed some major league help. My philosophy was simple. If you want to be a major league pitcher, you must work with a great pitching coach. If you want to be a good golfer, you have to get good lessons. If you are preparing for the NFL and you are looking to increase your speed, you should be working with speed and track specialists.

I sought to get these boys past the largest hurdle they had ever faced. I sought out to find the best. I found him in the most unlikely of places.

There was a guy on our East Lake Community Board named Comer Yates, who headed up the Atlanta Speech School. Comer was from a very storied Atlanta family. His father, Charlie Yates, had been good friends with Bobby Jones. His father respected Bob Jones and everything he stood for in life and the game of golf. Mr. Yates was also an accomplished golfer in his own right.

Charlie Yates was born in Atlanta on September 9, 1913. His impressive golf resume included winning the Georgia State Amateur in 1931 and 1932, the NCAA individual title in 1934, the Western Amateur title, and the coveted British Amateur Championship in 1938.

He had also been the low-scoring amateur while playing in the Masters, and he was named to multiple Walker Cup teams.

Also, like Jones, Yates had been a very successful businessman in Atlanta. The East Lake Community Foundation named their new golf course after him. Mr. Yates grew up in the East Lake neighborhood. He understood the true history of the area.

Comer and his brother, Charlie, had always been great to me. Comer had invited us over to his school in order to meet a guy whom Comer deemed one of the nation's best SAT experts.

I was initially skeptical, but after listening to the expert for a couple of hours I changed my mind. The expert was Larry Krieger. Larry was an A.P. art teacher from Princeton, New Jersey. He had been named the top A.P. art teacher in the world. Larry was amazing.

Larry talked about mixing and blending with all types of kids. He taught at Princeton High School, which was located down the street from Princeton University. He was a really funny guy. He was tall and lanky. His hair was always neat, but there were always a couple of hairs out of place like a mad scientist. He was also a little weird, but from my experience of working with young people, weird was always good. Larry was truly an amazing guy. I had never met anyone as serious about the SAT test as Larry. He was as serious about the SAT as I was about golf. He talked about putting SAT practice tests in the language of today's youth. This was the first concern, but I believed Larry was built for this.

He talked of shows with Paris Hilton and her cronies. He talked about other "white" shows that these kids never watched and had honestly never even heard of. The East Lake kids never watched these shows. I told Larry that in order to assimilate into their world, you have to get into their world. The East Lake students knew rap music, golf, the inner city, hip hop stars, and sports. Larry smiled and said he was going to figure out a way to reach them.

Larry gave us a great financial deal and the classes commenced. A year earlier he had tried his normal approach with students from Buckhead. Buckhead was a really affluent part of Atlanta. His quotidian method worked. But in order to bring it to East Lake, it needed some refinement and modification.

These classes went on for more than a year. The foundation supported my efforts to hire Larry. They set aside funds that we were able to use that allowed this miracle to take place. Larry would fly into Atlanta on a Saturday morning and we would work with the kids for about five or six hours on Saturday and Sunday. The boys really liked Larry and his approach. I would open up the school and Larry would become the "super" teacher. He would do his deal. Larry was also creatively stern. He demanded the attention of the boys. He used me in his class to help him with the boys. We actually made a good team, but I have always given Larry all of the credit. He was very flexible. He was the man!

Larry finally got to the boys. He read the 50 Cent autobiography; he started subscribing to *Vibe* magazine and a couple of urban publications. He started watching Black Entertainment Television. The strangest thing happened. His methods worked.

It took the boys at least four times to take the test, but it worked. He didn't try to reteach 10 or 11 years of unlearned education. He taught them how to take the SAT. It worked. All of the boys made a qualifying score.

Larry had truly become a part of the East Lake family. We would chat when he wasn't instructing the guys. We talked a lot about life. I shared with him what was going on in the lives of the boys.

He helped us research colleges. He wanted to be sure that the scores we sought would indeed get them in. I probably liked Larry because he went to the University of North Carolina. I was a Tar Heel at heart being from Winston-Salem. We definitely shared a lot of basketball stories.

The success of these boys actually went against all odds. It was also another example of the power of God. I felt as though God had his holy hand around this entire process. Some of these families were fighting an uphill battle at birth. God was truly rising up the valleys and leveling the mountains for black and brown people.

CHAPTER 15

Great Experiences

"Both riches and honor *come* from You, And You reign over all.
In Your hand *is* power and might; In Your hand *it is* to make
great and to give strength to all."

(1 Chron 29:12)

Shortly after I accepted the East Lake job in 1998, we took 45 children in our after-school program up to the Buford Fish Hatchery. The trip from East Lake to the hatchery was only about a 45-minute drive. Not knowing any better, I used the time to talk with the children about life, their families, vacations, special trips, etc. What I quickly learned was frightening, but not surprising.

To many of these children, driving out of downtown up Georgia 400 was a big deal. It was a vacation to some. I realized that the lack of exposure was not happenstance but due to socio-economic conditions. It was systemic, and if creative measures were not put in place, it would be cyclical. I leaned on the East Lake name and quickly tried to develop opportunities very similar to the ones I had experienced growing up in North Carolina. I traveled with the kids to local golf tournaments, the movies, and local NBA, NFL, NHL games. I invited local folks over to speak to the kids. I invited a local rap group (Goodie Mob) over to speak at the club, as I did with lawyers, doctors, judges, professional athletes, and other entertainers. I took the children to restaurants where they had to place napkins on their laps. I refrained from purchasing fast food during golf trips. I oftentimes picked their selections off the menu. They initially hated the food I ordered for them, but eventually they began to embrace it.

I worked very diligently to find professional people within Metro Atlanta who could volunteer and give a part of themselves to the kids.

As the golfers developed, I secured clothing among other things.

Based on my relationship with Coca-Cola, I was presented with an opportunity to take the children of my choice to respective Tiger Woods golf clinics all across the country. The kids participated and loved the opportunities.

I secured airline tickets for the entire program through Delta. I had developed a great friendship with Scarlett Brown. She was a former coworker of mine at the foundation and had moved on to bigger and better things at Delta. She was amazing. She also truly loved the kids. She never wanted to leave East Lake, but she noticed some financial discrepancies within the organization and accepted a better opportunity at the airlines. I also knew that in order to take advantage of all the support, I had to create an unbelievable product. I worked hard with these children on their golf games. They were able to occasionally break 80, but I wanted more.

I again went to one of my most trusted and admired volunteers, Valerie Levy. She told me about her personal golf instructor. She said his name was Mike Perpich and he was wonderful. I did my research and discovered that Mike was a master professional and also listed among the top 100 instructors in America in a couple of golfing publications. I also liked his style and demeanor. Mike was originally from Louisville. I had moved to Atlanta from Louisville. We knew a lot of the same people. Mike and his family were Christians. His beliefs and value system coincided with my beliefs and my value system.

Mike agreed to help. I asked him to help me advance my best golfers and help me prepare them for college. I knew we were several years away, but I also knew you could never start too soon.

Mike had worked with several PGA Tour players, LPGA players, and very good collegiate players. I knew he could help me. We worked out an arrangement and our goal of getting some boys to college worked.

I figured out that the easiest way to expand the world for these young people was to allow them to live in my world.

I took the boys to church with me and my family. I took them back to North Carolina with my family. They were included in my family cookouts. They met most of my buddies. I tried to encourage them to read some of the same books that I had enjoyed at their age. I studied with them. We searched the internet together. I made sure they had the collared golf shirts and the khaki pants and shorts. They were totally integrated as a part of my family. My family embraced this concept and they absolutely loved the guys.

CHAPTER 16

Neighborhood Kids

"Train up a child in the way he should go: and when he is old,
he will not depart from it."

(Proverbs 22:6)

The Governor is the affectionate name that I gave Willie Brown. Willie was the smoothest-talking and slickest fellow in the program. He had swag and a disposition that would lend well to survival in the streets. He didn't mind working, but he always wanted to figure out a way to increase each opportunity. He also grew to be six-foot-three, tall like his mom. I am not sure what was in the water in the neighborhood, but these kids grew to be very big. He was a good guy and very respectable.

I did learn one thing. Whenever Willie and my son teamed up, the game that these two played was always close to trouble. They often skirted the line that detailed right and wrong. Willie had an incredible golf swing. It was beautiful. Due to his skinny frame and height, he created a wide, smooth, Davis Love III-type arc during his take-back, and he created a tremendous amount of clubhead speed at impact. I believe that his physical stature was a huge advantage. The golf swing was almost flawless. His takeaway was slow and deliberate. He played a natural draw and he was fearless. All of his position lines were in sync.

He was not afraid to attack any pin on the course, and he definitely didn't mind gambling with his buddies.

Willie got good fast. He had exceptional hand-eye coordination, and his creativity around the greens was stellar. Willie had all of the intangibles to be an unbelievably good player. The only thing missing was the strong work ethic. He loved to play, but I never felt as though he was willing to "bleed" for the game. This would allow him to shoot in the mid-70s but hampered him from being a regular on the sub-70 circuit.

He was raised by a single mother. Tammy Brown had done everything in her power to position all of her kids for a better life. Willie was the next to the youngest and it was obvious that he had learned from the oldest children's mistakes. He was a true momma's boy.

Willie was never confrontational. He would huff and puff, but he wouldn't bite. He was harmless. He was incredibly social and he loved people. He could really read people, and his gauge for their attitudes and perceptions was pretty phenomenal. In most instances, I saw all of this as a huge positive, but there were a bevy of times when this was a huge negative. He took a lot of shortcuts in life. Instead of simply trying to find steady employment, he would try to sell bootleg CDs. Instead of studying like he was supposed to the night before, he would try to do a last-minute recap and fake his way through the assignments.

One of his funniest trying-to-be-slick moments happened when Willie was in Mrs. Manson's eighth grade class. Mrs. Manson was one of the old-school, gray-haired, black cat glasses-wearing, African-American, no-nonsense teachers who was still left in the APS system. She taught math and she didn't play. She was like your favorite grandmother who wasn't afraid to choke you out. She would always let me pop into her class unannounced. She and I had enjoyed a myriad of conversations about how to help the youth in East Atlanta. So, on this particular day, I snuck into the back door of her math class and she saw me, but Willie didn't. She always called him Mr. Brown. I wandered to an empty seat simply to observe. Then the fun began.

She was highlighting problems on the board and then said, "Mr. Brown, I want you to read the next question in the book and then verbally tell your golf instructor, who is in the back, how to work the problem." Willie turned rather quickly, along with most of the class, and gave me the head nod to acknowledge my presence. He turned back around in his seat and said, "Yes, ma'am." So now we are all waiting on Willie. Three minutes go by and he is staring intently into his book, but he isn't articulating anything. At about the six-minute mark, Mrs. Manson says, "Mr. Brown do you know how to solve the equation?" Willie said, "Yes, ma'am." At this point, I rose out of my super-small, LEGO-sized chair and walked over toward Willie's seat. I placed my hands on his shoulders and proceeded to help him. And then it hit me…dayyyyummmmmm.

Willie Brown had the book upside down. He was also on the wrong page. He had no idea what the hell was going on in the class. This was ridiculous and sad at the same time. I was trying to help make a way for this guy, but he wasn't helping himself. This was the slick part of him that pissed me off. This is why I had to stay on top of him. He was full of talent, but lazy.

He was forced to work a lot harder than some of the other guys because if ever confronted he thought he could sweet-talk his way out of it. In fact, Willie was close to being able to talk his way out of most things. The jail incident took life to another level and shut his verbiage down.

Another story that highlighted the depth of my plight was an incident at my house. On a Saturday afternoon, I took Willie and another student, Michael Bartholomew, over to my house to hang out with my son. Michael was also in the program, but he was a little older. The boys were outside playing ball when my wife called us all in for dinner. I noticed that Michael and Willie went in first. Michael basically just went in the house, went upstairs, and just went in my damn refrigerator. He looked in the cabinets and asked my wife what was on the dinner menu. It pissed me off, but it reiterated why I was trying to do what I was doing.

Michael would also show up late and try to always beat the system with his wit. I will never forget when he asked me if I received monthly food stamps. I told him no. He offered to sell me some. I mentioned that I thought the government had changed the way they allocated the "stamps." The government switched to a credit card system. He looked at me and laughed. He said, "Mr. Sam, I am from the hood." He said, "You know we can make anything work in our favor."

Michael was a great kid with a lot of rough edges. He is doing really well now in the United States Navy. One day while sitting in the golf office, I got a call on the phone. The voice on the other end said, "Mr. Sam, what's up? I bet you don't know who this is."

I instantly recognized the southern twang.

He said, "I just wanted to call to tell you thank you."

I said, "Thank me for what?"

He said, "I want to thank you for trying to help me." He said he wished he had listened more and maybe he would have gone to college.

I stopped him. I said, "Michael, you are doing really well for yourself." I told him that I was proud of him. I said, "God placed you exactly where you are supposed to be right now. You are on a big Navy vessel out in the ocean. God doesn't make mistakes." The phone was silent. We talked for a few more minutes before he hung up. But before he got off the phone he said, "By the way, I can still beat you in golf. I am the best golfer on the ship and I will always have enough game to beat you." I laughed and we eventually ended the call. That conversation was fuel for me to continue doing what I thought was right. Good things were happening and lives were being positively affected for the better.

CHAPTER 17

Rod (Spaceman)

"Foolishness [is] bound in the heart of a child; [but] the rod of correction shall drive it far from him."

(Proverbs 22:15)

Rod was one of the funniest kids I have ever met in my life. Imagine Chris Tucker, with his high-pitched voice, in a kid's body. That was Rod. Now imagine that voice at six-four, 200 pounds looking like Bob Marley with super-thick dreads. He was hilarious. He was the kid who would be walking up to the range and see a butterfly and might literally follow it, not realizing he was leaving the course. He would stand on a hill and cut a flip in the middle of the driving range. He was a great artist. He was very charming with a warm smile. He has a strong, religious mother and a few siblings. His older brother had gotten caught up in "Little Vietnam." His brother had sought a little neighborhood retaliation with an automatic weapon and is currently serving a lot of years, but you would never know that when dealing with Rod.

Rod's golf game had progressed because he wanted to be the best golfer in the program. At least he said he did, but you soon realized that he wasn't willing to put in the work. He loved to play but didn't love to practice. As he started to grow, the weirdest thing happened. He literally stopped playing golf. He just lost the passion. I think he started smelling himself. He was a good-looking kid and the girls loved him. This was a huge part of the problem. He was tall and good-looking. He also had a really easygoing disposition. He got a little bling in his ears and a platinum grill in his mouth. All of this attention ruined him. He was an average student in the classroom, but now school was also taking a back seat.

All of this madness came to a head during his junior year of high school. I think Rod saw the writing on the wall. He saw the other boys getting collegiate golfing opportunities. He also realized that he didn't have many options back in the neighborhood. He had worked enough with his uncle, who owned a moving company, moving furniture in the summer, that he soon realized he didn't want to work this hard for the rest of his life. We always talked about working smarter, not harder. A good education would help pave his way to a better life.

Studying became more of a priority. The driving range became his second home. He was showing up at SAT tutoring class on time for the first time. Things definitely changed back for the best. His golf scores came back and his SAT score increased with each try. He was now on the right track. I thought he had a mild case of ADD, but for now he was focused and doing all of the correct things.

Although the neighborhood housed some incredible characters, it was also blessed with some uber-talented kids. I tried to steer them all into golf, but I was smart enough to recognize that some of them might have been better suited to play other sports. Several of these students went on to play at big-time major universities. J.B. Holsey, Travis Leslie, Brandon Greene, and Brandon Watkins were four examples of neighborhood kids who played under the big lights.

Both J.B. and Travis had grown up and developed into exceptional athletes. They also developed into strong, intelligent young men. J.B. excelled in football and baseball, whereas Travis excelled in basketball.

J.B. had it tough. He was raised by his aunt. His mother was occasionally in the picture, but his aunt played the caregiver. His ability to throw a football and a baseball helped rearrange his sporting priorities.

J.B. had grown to about six-foot. He was long and wiry, but very fast. After completing his first year of high school at the neighborhood school, he got a creative break and switched schools. This seemed to happen to all of the best athletes in the community. They all ended up going to high schools in other parts of Atlanta. They were basically recruited.

His new high school was quickly becoming a football power. With J.B., Grady High School had received a kid who possessed a 98-mph fastball, could throw a football 80 yards from a standstill position, and recorded a 4.4 time in the 40-yard dash. He was also a hard-working student. We often discussed college. We always talked about life. I knew he would make it because he was mentally stronger than the average kid. His mother had run across a lot of issues in the streets and nothing ever came easy.

While at Grady, he became one of the top quarterbacks in the country. His high school football team was ranked No. 1 in the state in its respective class. He had improved his grade point average to 3.2. After verbally committing to play quarterback at the University of Nebraska, he changed his mind at the last minute and decided to go to South Dakota State University. Mississippi State, LSU, Clemson, and a host of other schools had wanted his football services. The thought of Coach Nick Saban sitting in his kitchen eating a fried chicken dinner coupled with mac and cheese trying to convince J.B. to join him at LSU is still one of my fondest memories. He spurned all of the big boys, but he definitely decided against Nebraska after the university fired then head coach Frank Solich. Solich had just completed a very successful 8-3 campaign, but had gotten busted for a DUI.

J.B. was also one of the best baseball prospects in the country. After the completion of his senior year, he competed in the U.S. All-American game, in which he went 3-for-4 at the plate and struck out 10 batters. He was drafted and signed with the Anaheim Angels out of high school. Things were great! Or were they…

J.B.'s high school baseball coach got pissed off because he'd refused to pitch during a game, due to an injury. The coach told all of the major league teams that J.B. was going to give up baseball. This was totally not true. J.B.'s true love was baseball. The misinformation prompted his stock to drop in the MLB Draft from a sure third-rounder to a 19th-rounder. This equated to a lot of missed zeros on the end of his signing bonus. This was also important because the Angels were paying for his college education. This was money out of his pocket. This was important too because J.B. had come from nothing. The more money he was able to get up front, the more money he would be able to save on the back end.

His closest circle of influence let him down. The people around him manipulated him into attending South Dakota State. The word on the street was that five people around him, including his high school coach, got paid $50,000 each when he decided to attend SDSU. I told J.B. when he was a kid that I would never make any decisions for him. I wanted him to realize the importance of decisions and, therefore, he made all of his decisions. Although I was willing to advise him, I only wanted to play the part of a silent partner. I enjoyed staying in the background. I would only offer certain opinions if I were consulted.

One day we invited representatives for the Atlanta Braves over to the golf club to discuss J.B.'s options. We sat quietly, allowing the professionals to sketch out their plans for J.B.'s path to the major leagues. I allowed J.B. to control the meeting. Although we talked before going into the meeting, I wanted him to realize the future was his and not mine. The people around him in high school tried to sabotage his future. This isn't super unusual because most people are selfish. The Bible says, "No one should seek their own good, but the good of others." J.B. would later admit to me that he thought a couple of grown folks around him had accepted up to $50,000 respectively for his college decision. His comments confirmed the rumors that had circulated through the neighborhood for years. This crushed him. I remember on one occasion he mentioned that the head coach at SDSU mentioned his reluctance in trusting people. Now you know why. It is sad that some people place a financial responsibility on a child's head unknowingly.

Travis Leslie's story was very similar to many others in the community. His mother was a strong person and a hard worker. She constantly worked overtime to provide for him and his two siblings. He was also steered away from the neighborhood in order to attend an out-of-district high school. Travis developed into a superstar on the court. He made the local all-star teams and he too was paired with some of the best talent in the country in high school. Travis' story also illustrates the power or influence that some coaches possess. J.B.'s coach was a negative turnoff, whereas Travis relied on his coach. His coach played an integral part in where he went to college, and the influence helped his decision on how long to stay in college before turning pro. Although his coach was controlling, I think he helped Travis a lot.

For most of his young life, his legs were a lot longer than his arms. We used to tease him all the time and tell him that his body better grow in proportion or he would be a funny-looking old man. Travis would often stand out on the driving range hitting golf shots, but he would be talking and thinking about basketball. I will never forget the one day I was probing him, trying to get a golf-specific answer out of him. I finally asked Travis about his future plans. He looked me in my eyes and said, "Mr. Sam, one day I am going to play in the NBA." I didn't know what to say but okay. I would never burst a kid's bubble because I know dreams actually do come true. I was proof of it, but I was also realistic in my approach. I knew none of his basketball dreams would come without hard work, dedication, and some God-given size. I was thinking that he better grow to be at least six-four or six-five simply to get a shot.

I remember one day the guys left the golf course and went over to the YMCA to play some hoops. In the midst of all of the whoofing and trash talking, Travis caught the ball out on a fast break and Rod made the fatal mistake of trying to block his shot. Rod could jump. He was long and lean and was slightly taller than Travis. Travis raised up and the rest has become East Lake lore. Rod got a facial treatment at a young age. For the record, Travis was only in the seventh grade. We were definitely laughing at Rod, but this only reminded us that Travis might be special.

After graduating from Columbia High School in Atlanta, Travis went on to play at the University of Georgia. He left college early and became a second-round draft pick by the Los Angeles Clippers. One of his collegiate highlights that is still a YouTube sensation was "the dunk." He had given me tickets to the game at Rupp Arena in Lexington, Kentucky. It was always a thrill going to watch him play. During the game, after a Kentucky missed basket, Travis got out on a fast break and realized that only one defender, DeMarcus Cousins, could challenge him at the rim. Cousins positioned himself to try to take a charge and subsequently got posterized. DeMarcus Cousins got a Rod experience. Travis raised up as if he had wings and put his waist in Cousins' mouth. Boof! Travis smashed on him hard. He got in him. This was a great dunk. In today's technological age, it can definitely be Googled. I guess Travis knew more than the rest of us. But he really didn't. God steered these steps. God made these dreams come true!

There were others who grew up in East Lake who made it out to do some pretty special things. James Davis, who went on to star at Clemson as a running back, eventually moved on to the NFL. Brandon Watkins (West Virginia University, basketball), Brandon Greene (University of Alabama, Chicago Bears, Carolina Panthers), Sheddrict Zellner (rapper), and many more wonderfully talented young people were all raised in this community. Shawty Lo (rapper) even had a son in my golf program. As the neighborhood continued to improve, a torrent of students began attending some of the best universities in the country not just due to sports, but also academics. The neighborhood school evolved from the worst in the Atlanta Public School System to the number one ranked school in the APS system.

CHAPTER 18

Tour Championship Week

"For we are his workmanship, created in Christ Jesus unto good works, which God hath before ordained that we should walk in them."

(Ephesians 2:10)

In 1998, when the PGA Tour decided to associate itself with East Lake, my boss asked me to come up with a few ideas or create a few ways that we could use the tournament to expose our children.

The first two concepts that I came up with became permanent mainstays. I started the concept of what I deemed "Caddy for a Day." This concept would allow me an opportunity to select 30 kids from my program. They would walk with the 30 participating professionals during the Tuesday practice round at the PGA Tour Championship. The Tour Championship presents the richest purse on Tour, and the tournament is only for the top 30 players on the PGA Tour. The tournament is now the last stop of the FedEx Cup. This tourney now determines the FedEx Cup champion, which is determined after the culmination of a year's worth of points.

I would have two adults stationed at holes 11 and 6. The front and back sides of the course are now reversed. They would introduce each student to their respective golfer. The students would have an opportunity to walk the par-3 hole with the professional. My thought was simple. I was hoping each golfer would talk with their respective child. I was also hoping that each golfer would give each child a chance to carry their bag or hit a shot.

Well, this was the first time on the Tour that something like this had happened. It started slow, but by the end of the day it totally worked.

I had also tried to take into consideration that some professionals might not be very receptive of this concept. I had also invited 30 of our regular volunteers to accompany the children for the duration of the day. I paired one volunteer with one child. The event far exceeded my expectations.

Payne Stewart, Bob Tway, Tom Lehman, David Toms, Stewart Cink, Fred Funk, Chris DeMarco, Davis Love, and Tiger Woods, simply to name a few, were all really wonderful with the kids. In fact, they were all great. Payne Stewart and Bob Tway gave the children a quick lesson, but they also let the students hit the club of their choice from their bag. In most instances, the clubs were as long as the kids were tall.

The second created event has truly been special. This was also an opportunity for us to highlight the Charlie Yates Golf Course.

I utilized Mike Perpich, my teaching guru, along with the help of Ron Cross, who was the tournament director at the time. It took some last-minute conversations with Mike in the locker room dealing with the professionals, but it worked. Mike had experience working with several Tour professionals. He understood their pulse.

I paired five professionals on the same team with three kids from my program. It created a Ryder Cup format. I dressed every team in the same colored shirts. The professionals played their own ball and the kids played a captain's choice. As the event matured and my best golfers got better, I allowed them to challenge the professionals shot for shot.

Both events made the local news and the front page of sports in the *Atlanta Journal-Constitution*. These events also helped me keep Brandon,

Shelton, Rod, and Willie on track. It made them practice. It also showed them that it was okay to be different. Golf was cool. It showed them that a pot at the end of the golfing rainbow did exist.

But more importantly, it allowed these boys to develop relationships with the world's best golfers.

CHAPTER 19
Tom Lehman

"By their fruit you will recognize them. Do people pick grapes from thorn bushes, or figs from thistles?"

(Matthew 7:16)

My relationship with PGA Tour star Tom Lehman was special. During one Tour Championship, Tom told me before he left Atlanta that he would love to help. I took him up on his offer. I asked him if we could do lunch when he came to Georgia to participate in the Masters the following year. He came up to East Lake and I took him to lunch. I stressed to him that Shelton, Eric, Brandon, Willie, Rod, and a few others had really taken to the game and that I thought that they were getting close enough to potentially earn a collegiate scholarship. I also said that the most urgent need for the program was good equipment. Tom asked me to tell him what I needed and he would make it happen. He was true to his word.

When I first moved to Atlanta, I met a very successful businessman named Don Patterson. Don's daughter had been a standout junior golfer. She consequently accepted a great golf scholarship from a Southeastern Conference school. Don was a Christian. He was heavily involved in the Fellowship of Christian Athletes program. We talked a lot about Tom

Lehman. Don told me that when Tom was on the mini-tours trying to create a name for himself, he would allow Tom to stay with him to help cut expenses. Don talked about Tom's Christian background and his beliefs.

While talking with Tom, I reflected on these conversations and I knew God had ordered his steps. I have always been a huge believer in divine intervention. I am a big believer that everything happens for a reason.

I instantly became a major Tom Lehman fan. Tom did exactly what he said he would do. One of his largest sponsors was TaylorMade. A couple weeks later, several sets of TaylorMade irons showed up at my office. I knew the process worked. He actually remembered all of the kids. He truly went out of his way to make a difference.

Special events were also taking place during the Tour Championship inside of the community school. With the help of several volunteers, I was able to create a golf library within Drew Charter School. Drew Charter School, which was owned and operated by the East Lake Community Foundation, was quickly turning into one of the best schools in Atlanta. I had spoken to one of my board members, who happened to be a great national writer, and asked him for his help.

I first met Chris Milliard back in 1992 while I was interning at *Golf Digest Magazine*. Chris wrote for *Golf World*. Both publications shared the same building. Based on his experience, I had guessed that he had maintained his national contacts in the writing industry. These contacts could only help the book collecting. Chris had worked with some of the best. I was correct in my assertion. Chris helped me get letters out to well-known and respected authors and companies and the books began pouring in. I confided in Chris that my fire and passion for the game had been fueled by my desire to read about the game and my zest to learn its history.

Drew Charter gave me an actual section in their library. I asked Turner Sports to donate a couple of computers for this special golf section. We also placed large black golf history exhibits on the walls. The golf exhibit had been contracted out through the Atlanta History Center. It depicted black golf in Georgia, which was highlighted by Lee Elder's feat of being the first black person to play in the Masters. The space inside of the library was amazing. The section contained more than 500 golf books for all grade levels. I also received several books that collectors told me were valued at more than $1,000 respectively. In order to change people's lives, it has to be done through education. Reading is truly fundamental. Many years earlier, slaves were killed and maimed for trying to learn how to read. Reading had been locked behind closed book covers. The students at Drew Charter were now being given the keys. The future was now within their reach.

CHAPTER 20

My Family

"Call unto me, and I will answer thee, and show thee great
and mighty things, which thou knowest not."

(Jeremiah 33:3)

"Do you sacrifice one and save the rest or do
you do nothing and lose them all?"

Friedrich Nietzsche

Accepting the job at East Lake was an easy adjustment for me, but I didn't know about the impact it would have on my family. I realized that I was going to need all the support from Allison, Cameron, Brooke, and Tony that they could muster if I was going to be able to do what needed to be done.

I was traveling a lot, going in really early in the morning, bringing the boys home to my house, taking them on vacations with my family, playing golf with them during my downtime, taking them to church and school supply shopping, etc. It wasn't a job. It was my calling. I had made it my purpose, my mission to see these boys through to the end. It was my ministry. Although they weren't my biological children, they were "truly" family.

In order to fully integrate the neighborhood with my family, I enrolled my son Tony into the same elementary school with these guys. The school in the neighborhood was underperforming, but I was naive enough to think I could fix everything. Although Tony was a year younger, I hoped he would be a positive influence on some of the neighborhood kids. Hell, I figured out later that he was the ringleader to most of the mischief.

My wife Allison was incredibly bright. I would say that when it comes to the mastery of the written word, she was one of the best. She had a wonderful job as a marketing guru. We had a great family schematic when we moved to Atlanta, but I could feel the paradigm begin to shift.

The job was creating subtle tremors in the marriage, and little did I know that a full-fledged earthquake was on the horizon. She felt as if I were spending an abundance of time with the East Lake children. In fact, she thought I was shortchanging her.

Although she was well within her power to voice her concerns, her assertions were incorrect. We were spending a lot of time together as a family, but we had a crazy marriage. Our issues ran deeper than me simply working with young people. We started going to different churches. The attention monster was starting to rear its head. Several of my non-trusting issues were rising to the surface. We were falling apart at the seams, which was making the day-to-day communications very difficult to navigate. I loved her and I am sure she felt the same way, but we had a few insurmountable issues. I had always felt that she was jealous of me. Many years later she would confirm that she had been competing with me. We got along great most times, but there were times when tension at the house would become unbearable.

Marriages aren't competitions. Marriages take a lot of work, forgiveness, and understanding. They are very delicate partnerships filled with a lot of love, compassion, and a bevy of complexity. The Bible says, "Love suffereth long, and is kind; love envieth not; love vaunteth not itself, is not puffed up, doth not behave itself unseemly, seeketh not its own, is not provoked, taketh not account of evil; rejoiceth with the truth;

beareth all things, believeth all things, hopeth all things, endureth all things."

She deserved the notoriety because of her skill-set, but unfortunately, she wasn't in athletics or an industry that received headlines. I never sought the attention. I sought results through executing processes. I would have preferred to stay behind the scenes.

In reality, I probably did spend an excessive amount of time with the East Lake youth, but I always included my children. My children were involved in most of these unique experiences. I also tried to include my wife. The trips to the NCAA national championship games, trip to Bermuda, the Masters, trip to Scotland, collegiate and professional games, and concerts were enjoyed by the entire family. Both sets of kids needed me, but they needed me in different ways. Serving as their golf instructor was secondary. I loved my three children. I tried feverishly to create a balance with my kids because I knew the journey with the East Lake youth would also teach them some valuable lessons.

Tony was becoming a pretty good athlete. He was tall, but very lean. He needed to bulk up. He was also really bright. He wanted to give up playing golf so that he could pursue his dream of playing collegiate football. He wanted to emulate his Uncle Eric and play on the gridiron. Brooke was developing into a beautiful young lady, but she was also a really talented basketball player. Cameron was a brand-new baby so she was living the dream.

My wife and I often argued over the assertion that I was taking my children for granted. We simply had to agree to disagree. This was a very tough time for us. I knew in my heart of hearts that I was doing what God was telling me to do. God had ordered my steps and I knew I had to remain obedient. But many of our differences were also attributable to our very different upbringings. My parents worked with children for a living. My parents gave most of themselves to others. Allison's mother worked with children and her father was a financial guy. Her parents were wonderful people, but the dynamic was different. The biggest difference was age. They were 10 years older than my parents and I am sure this created our different set of expectations. Age has a way of making people see things through a different set of lenses. Again, I related a lot to upbringing. I wasn't being selfish. I knew my children needed me, but I also knew that the East Lake kids didn't have many alternatives.

The entire ordeal and the subsequent move to California essentially highlighted that I should have worked harder to understand Allison at home. I held my wife accountable for her work with the children, but I was also spreading myself too wide and too thin. This allowed me to help a multitude of people, but it splintered my relationship at home. I had been willing to make the tough sacrifice. My minor in college was philosophy and it had prepared me for this moment in my life.

One of the main people we studied a lot in Dr. Monmarquet's class at TSU was Nietzsche, who was heavily influenced by Aristotle. Nietzsche held women and children in very high regard. He said, "All things are subject to interpretation, whichever interpretation prevails at a given time, is a function of power and not truth. On the mountains of truth, you can never climb in vain: either you will reach a point higher up today, or you will be training your powers so that you will be able to climb higher tomorrow." I wanted to save all of the kids, but I knew climbing that mountain would be difficult. They needed someone with a high moral and ethical code. This came natural to me because this is how I was raised and it was in my DNA. I watched my parents bail students out of jail and testify for them in court. My parents shared themselves with seemingly everyone. I was only mimicking a certain behavior. I guess Allison was doing the same. This proved to be a ridiculous ongoing battle that I was prepared to fight. We fought and fought. I won the battle, but lost the war. We eventually divorced, but the lives of the East Lake youth were enhanced in the process. I never allowed my personal life to affect my professional life. I was able to organize, prioritize, and compartmentalize the respective aspects of my life.

I have always felt that my children would be a lot better off because of their relationship with the East Lake children. It is difficult to find a book that teaches your kids to give of themselves to others. A clinched fist can't help anyone. They were experiencing a lesson in giving firsthand. Experience has always been the best teacher.

My children and I realized the enormity of our project and conceptualized several important realisms that the East Lake children already knew and lived on a daily basis.

Realisms the East Lake Way:

- Money doesn't grow on trees
- Be willing to work for something instead of always asking
- Tomorrow is not promised
- Be extremely thankful for what you have and what you have received
- The little things matter
- Live, plan, live, plan
- Parents are not obligated to do anything for you but die when it is their time
- Be willing to forgive, and understand some folks know not what they do
- It is okay to be skeptical; it helps keep people on their toes
- Parents are doing their best; they were not presented with a manual at your birth
- At the end of the day, we have to trust someone
- No man is an island; no one can make it in this world alone
- Champions are made on a thousand mornings when no one is watching

I always thought my family could learn as much from East Lake as East Lake could learn from us. Finding a delicate balance was difficult at times. This is perhaps the major reason why I tried to mix the two. Both of my parents had spent their entire working lives working in the educational system. My father had been a principal for 20 years, an assistant principal for 10 years, and a teacher for four years. My dad spent 34 years in the educational system. My mom was a high school English teacher and subsequently became a college professor. She taught for more than 35 years. This was unequivocally my training and preparation for my future trade.

I can remember when I was in elementary school and my mother was a softball coach at one of the eight high schools in Winston-Salem. On game days, my mom's students would come by the elementary school to sign me out. This would never be possible today. The advent of the crazy school shooter around the U.S. changed all of this. You have to now get buzzed into a school building and it practically takes a presidential executive order to check a student out of school. Many of our trusting behaviors are a thing of the past.

My mom's students picking me up at school allowed me to attend the games and ride the high school bus with the team. I honestly don't remember any of the actual game results, but I do remember the process. I remember students coming by the house for meals, students coming by and calling for money, students calling in need of help. This continued even after many of these students left high school and matriculated to college.

My dad's scenario was no different. I remember him loaning out money, getting a gun pulled on him at Parkland High School, and having a brick thrown at him at South Park. My dad was a counselor to some and a father figure to most. My parents were teachers, counselors, food providers, co-parents, and mental health officials to their students.

I remember when one of my mother's students had an opportunity to play football at an ACC institution. He needed a lot of extra help getting into college. My mother tutored him after school. The student's mother was very appreciative. The student subsequently passed his SATs and qualified to play. After four great years in college, he was drafted into the NFL and was a standout receiver for nine years. Both of his younger brothers also received the extra assistance and it also culminated in great NFL careers for them as well.

These are some of the stories of my upbringing. I always thought the service lifestyle was the normal reality. My parents expected and demanded this mindset out of all the teachers and coaches who worked with me. I grew up thinking that everyone who dealt with kids was supposed to sacrifice for the cause, as it related to our youth. This is exactly how I treated the East Lake youth. Your phone was always on, the door was always open, and your best foot was always forward.

This belief was not universally embraced. I also realized early that some of the teachers in the lives of these kids were only seeking a check and could truly care less about where these students ended up. I never felt like my boys ever truly garnered the basics or fundamentals.

I think the teachers cared more about all of the neighborhood kids staying out of jail than mastering the King's English. This is why I respected the kids so much. They are constantly saying, "Mr. Sam, I want to be like you when I grow up." It is truly flattering, but I always tried to convey to the students that the respect was mutual.

I respected their starting point and I also respected their path. They had started life from behind. The race started without them. This is when the realisms hit me. I realized that they were indeed my heroes. These students were walking down paths that had never been paved. They were the trendsetters in their families. I always felt a little empathy for the kids and their families, but the best way to describe my true emotions would be that of an advocate. I vowed in the beginning that I would help level their playing fields. I realized how hard their families were working simply to keep the heat and the lights on. I vowed to pick up the slack in the educational department. I did this through school visits. I went by their schools at least twice a week to check on their progress. I wanted to make sure the boys realized that Mr. Sam could pop up at any time. I felt like it would keep them on their toes and it would help hold them accountable. I wanted the schools to know that these kids needed their support, but also that these students had some outside support. This held their teachers accountable. The teachers were very receptive. They would let me come and sit in on their classes. Some of the teachers called me regularly with updates and some went a step further and sent regular emails. The process of overseeing the system worked. All of this proved vital as the boys neared the end of high school and prepared for college.

Ms. Brown, Ms. Davis, Ms. Lowry, Ms. Bradley, and many of the other parents were all pleased, but at the same time very hopeful that the process would indeed work. These families were now a cemented part of my family. I love family. I had made their mission a very personal mission of mine.

CHAPTER 21

Worst Decision

"For the time is coming when people will not endure sound teaching, but having itching ears they will accumulate for themselves teachers to suit their own passions."

(2 Timothy 4:3)

I have always prided myself in helping folks. I bugged the head of the foundation in the beginning about hiring an assistant and my persistence finally paid off. I hired a guy whom I knew. I played collegiate golf with him. He had grown up down in the country town of Jackson, Tennessee. He had been showered with a lot of love from his grandmother and mother. He believed in discipline. We didn't agree on everything, but the philosophical concepts came easy. He was an athlete. He had been raised playing a variety of sports. This was also important because most of the kids in the neighborhood played football, basketball, and golf. I am a huge proponent of playing multiple sports. Each sport helps to develop different muscle groups along with different physical and mental skills. I thought the biggest advantage to this hire was his background. "Big" Nyre had been essentially raised by a single "parent," his grandmother. I thought this would help him readily identify with the kids in the neighborhood.

With his hire, we increased our numbers and increased the number of times we could offer golf to the outside world. The numbers had increased from about 50 students in the beginning to several hundred. The East Lake Junior Academy was booming.

This was also beginning to happen nationally. The First Tee National School Program had patterned its junior golf program after the East Lake Junior Golf Academy, utilizing many of its concepts and principles. Programs were sprouting up all over the country and other parts of the world. This hire also allowed me to offer golf six days a week and it afforded me an opportunity to focus on fundraising and developing the youth in the program.

The First Tee of Nashville offered me a unique opportunity to leave East Lake, but I knew the time wasn't right. I also professed my belief that God would prepare me to leave when the time was proper. I told Nashville about my assistant. They trusted me and they offered "Big" Nyre the job. He accepted the job and he subsequently left for Tennessee.

This was great on a personal level, but on a professional level it left me in a "good" quandary. I was now going to have to find someone who loved children, someone who could relate to their plight, but also someone who had the golf acumen to help them become proficient golfers.

I did a national search and finally offered the job to A.J. Bronson. A.J. was unemployed, but he had served as the head of a PGA facility in Massachusetts, and he had served as a head golf professional and collegiate coach out in Montana. I knew that he had lost a couple of jobs because of run-ins with management, but I thought the overriding love for children would outweigh any negative.

I had a lot of family in Chicago. I had read a lot about A.J.'s father in national economic publications. His father had been the first black CEO of a major bank in Chicago. According to CNN, a lot of folks didn't like him because he wasn't afraid to challenge the system and he didn't back down from controversy, but the underserved loved him. He donated millions of dollars to schools around the United States. He believed that everyone deserved a financial chance. People didn't like him because he didn't hold his tongue. I think that is why I liked him. He challenged the status quo. He stood up to the establishment. There always had to be the "change police." The world needs instigators. Like his dad, A.J. enjoyed economics. A.J. would later leave Atlanta and move back to Chicago to get into the banking business. He eventually became the CEO of a small community-driven bank on the North Side. This actually gave them a pretty unique distinction as the first black, father-son CEO tandem in the state of Illinois.

A.J. was older than me. He was a pretty good instructor and a good golfer. He constantly talked about several of his students who were doing well on the mini-tours. Many years earlier, while serving as an assistant golf coach at Montana State, he caught a nice recruiting trend and found some incredibly talented youth who helped Montana State win consecutive national championships. I thought A.J. would truly be a positive influence on the boys. He had recently gone through a divorce, and I knew he needed the income. He told me that he loved working with children. He constantly lamented on their importance in his life. He brought along some creative baggage, but I honestly thought everything was cool. The East Lake boys needed positive mentors. They needed an additional body on the range until dark. They needed their swings examined on a regular basis. A.J. became very friendly with the boys. They spent time at his house. He took them shopping and helped them execute their errands. A.J. filled the personal friend role, but the professional void was never filled. I quickly learned that A.J. simply wanted a paycheck. He wasn't interested in teaching juniors that didn't display a passion for the game. This was a problem. East Lake was full of children who loved life, but a lot of children don't love the game of golf. It makes sense.

The crux of these children were products of families who had never been exposed to golf. Most parents in the neighborhood had never touched a golf club. Golf is a game that has to be massaged. It has to be nurtured and it takes time. The one thing that I constantly stressed to A.J. was the fact that we had to help the students nurture their love for the game. We were working with a lot of "good" children. There are a lot of positive results that can happen when children are acclimated to the game of golf. The major purpose was not to create an abundance of professional golfers, but to create an abundance of positive and professional people. They would potentially be members of local country clubs, lawyers, small business owners, architects, golf course designers, educators, publishers, and authors. There were more advantages to working with the non-interested than only the interested. The percentage of golfers who actually make it out on tour is far less than one percent. These are very small odds and I don't think any of these statistics interested A.J. The weirdest part about all of this is that the best golfers didn't improve. Their scores remained the same and the time he spent with them waned. I honestly just think he lost his way. When life deals us oranges, we can only make orange juice. When life gives us lemons, we can only squeeze out lemonade. I think A.J. wanted orange juice, but he had a bushel of apples and watermelon thoughts.

He wasn't on the range with the boys much. A.J. had developed a great relationship with the head pro. They were both consumed with giving additional lessons. These lessons created a ton of extra revenue for the professional staff. This is absolutely understandable for the average golf professional, but in East Lake the head professional was salaried and nicely compensated. A.J. was also compensated really well. A.J. and the pro seemed to form a tag team of opposition against the kids. They were very negative. They complained privately about the kids' appearances and their nice golf equipment, and they seemed to be filled with hate. We call these folks crabs. People are so quick to blame persons of other races for their problems and all they need to do is take a quick look in the mirror. The man in the mirror always exposes the truth. A lot of parents and others in the neighborhood who knew the two of them called them haters. They were silent assassins. They were quick to smile in your face, but they would cut you deep as soon as you turned around.

A.J. was also constantly absent from his responsibility. He spent a lot of time in the school hanging around certain, attractive, single female teachers. The kids were pushed to the side.

It was weird. I also needed him to support the program at the course, but it never developed. The pros at the Yates Course totally mistreated the boys. They talked trash to the kids, threatened to remove their golf course privileges, cut back on their hours of work at the golf course (Rod, Willie, Eric, Brandon, and Shelton all had part-time jobs working at Charlie Yates Golf Course), and used their golf equipment, which was stored in the golf clubhouse's closet, without their permission. The boys were not totally absolved, but again they were kids. The boys were doing some things around the course that they shouldn't have been doing. They played in fivesomes, wore jeans on the course, and shot dice in the caddy barn. They weren't angels. A.J. constantly chided the boys in front of the adults in the clubhouse. He constantly referenced the kids' personal situations, their academic progression (school didn't come easy to some of the boys), their clothing preferences, and how they presented themselves.

A.J. sought to pacify everyone who wanted pacification. He simply didn't have any leadership skills. I had hired a "friend" for the boys, but this turned into a huge minus. The kids needed structure. They needed discipline. They needed to be led by the adults in their circles. They didn't need any more friends. It was tough. He was great when I micro-managed him, but when I left him in charge, the kids didn't get what they needed the most. All things aside, there was one incident that really worried me. It left me befuddled and reiterated that I needed some more help.

CHAPTER 22

Neighborhood Crazy

"And in their greed they will exploit you with false
words. Their condemnation from long ago is not idle,
and their destruction is not asleep."

(2 Peter 2:3)

The golf course was a safe haven for the entire neighborhood. Regardless of my efforts, I realized kids were still going to be kids. Although they made tremendous strides in school and in life, they were still kids. Kids do some dumb things. They would try to come out and play with T-shirts on. Naw…I wasn't going to let that slide. They couldn't say they didn't have golf gear. I had gotten them all a ton of nice golf gear. They would start talking trash and, in an effort to settle it, go out and play late in the day as a five-some. The course hated this. They knew fivesomes weren't allowed.

Other times, they would all aim for the range picker and try to blast the cart. They also got caught gambling in the back of the cart barn. Eric Davis and the boys were literally sitting on the ground shooting dice. Bananas! These were all things that they could control. When they did the correct thing, I praised them, and when they did wrong, I laid into them.

There was one incident that I think truly took the cake.

One evening when we were leaving the golf course, all hell broke loose. Shelton asked Dre about his cash. "Hey, Dre. Do you have my money?" he asked. Dre was one of the assistant professionals at the course.

Dre laughed and snapped back, "No, you didn't play all 18 holes."

Dre was referring to a bet that he had made with Shelton the previous day. Dre had bet Shelton that he couldn't beat Willie over at East Lake on the big course. Betting was not uncommon for the boys. They loved to gamble. These boys would bet anybody. They would bet each other on the course all the time. They knew where I stood on gambling, but I knew that boys would be boys. I actually read somewhere years ago that older golf PGA Tour legends including Jack Nicklaus thought that kids gambling on the course actually made them better golfers by increasing their focus.

I don't gamble because of a junior golfing incident I experienced as a kid. I had also told Dre not to bet with the boys. My explanation to him was simple. These kids worked too hard for the little money that they did have and I didn't want them to lose it over a ridiculous bet. I felt like I had to help them help themselves. It was crazy, but it was real. Nevertheless, the badgering continued and it only got worse.

Dre said, "You only played 13 holes."

Shelton stopped and said, "Man, you are trippin'. Man, we had to stop because it got dark. I was up 5 when we quit."

Dre said, "Well too bad. I ain't payin' you."

Shelton laughed and said, "We'll see." Shelton laughed and walked out. He abruptly walked out and stooped down to pick up a handful of dirt. This is when everything went nuts.

Shelton walked out into the parking lot and placed the dirt onto Dre's nice, clean Honda Civic. The Honda was hooked up nicely with a great set of rims. Dre loved his car. He kept his Civic clean. You would swear he owned a Bentley. Dre's smile turned into a frown. Dre sprang out of the golf shop and confronted Shelton. By this time, the other boys were laughing hysterically. They were laughing for a lot of reasons. They first knew how much Dre loved his car. They were also laughing because they were sick and tired of Dre and Paul, the head professional, picking on and "hating" on them. The other boys also felt that Dre was a big bully, but the difference was simple. Shelton wasn't afraid of him and he wouldn't back down from the fat "yellow" man. Dre was a light-skinned black guy.

Now Dre was huffing and puffing and the other boys were literally laughing uncontrollably. Little did they know, this laughter was totally infuriating Dre. He was becoming incensed. He saw the dirt as total disrespect. The kids didn't care. None of them respected Dre and Paul because they talked down to the kids. The boys could care less. They always said, "We are not studding those haters." They always said that Dre and Paul were jealous of the clothing, travel, privileges, and equipment they received. This was true. Paul and Dre were always commenting about the equipment that the young boys owned. They would say that the boys didn't deserve it. They complained that they got too much for free. They felt they should have to pay. They constantly talked about their life as kids. I listened, but I always reminded the grown folks that their beginning points in this world were so much different than these neighborhood boys. Dre and Paul had two working parents. The boys didn't.

I had it set up so that the boys could leave their golf equipment in the clubhouse in a secure closet. Only Paul and his staff had access to the closet. I would come in and Paul and Dre would be out on the range hitting balls with the boys' equipment. After I left the job for Stanford, Shelton's driver was stolen out of his bag in the closet. The golf course informed Shelton that no one was going to replace the missing Titleist driver. Shelton called me in California and I sent him a new one. Of course, this pissed the haters off, but too bad. They made sure to tell the boys to call their "daddy" whenever they needed something, yet they were actually living in Atlanta interacting with the boys on a daily basis. They referred to me as the boy's dad. It was intended as a negative and a low blow. I saw it as a positive. The boys were awesome.

The entire time that Dre and Shelton were screaming at each other, the rest of the staff was standing around laughing with the other kids.

They never made any attempt to intervene.

Dre quickly chirped that since Shelton placed the dirt on the car, he was going to break all of Shelton's clubs, which were in the golf clubhouse closet. Shelton turned and quickly walked into the clubhouse to get his clubs. Brandon scurried to beat Dre inside. Dre followed and abruptly locked the door behind them. Now, Dre has cornered Shelton one-on-one in an empty clubhouse. They were now shouting expletives back and forth. Brandon was watching through the front door, reassuring Dre that this could turn into his biggest nightmare. These neighborhood guys were prepared to fight Dre and kick his butt.

I also forgot to mention that the aforementioned bet was over $1. To Shelton, $1 meant something on the value meal menu at McDonald's. To Dre, $1 was nothing. Things get crazy in the hood. These young people had kicked the victim title off of their resume and now they were willing to confront anyone or anything that was not good for their future. This is just one crazy example of hood life.

CHAPTER 23
Scotland

"His divine power has granted to us all things that pertain
to life and godliness, through the knowledge of Him
who called us to His own glory and excellence."

(2 Peter 1:3)

We were in Atlanta boarding an evening plane heading to the 2005 British Open. We were sitting in First Class on Delta and laughing, saying how can two boys from East Lake, which the boys referred to as the "ghetto" or Zone 6, get to go to the British Open. Atlanta is broken down into zones, and popular rappers have glorified many of the undesirable events or acts that take place within the respective zones. For many, the zones are an inner-city rite of passage.

The reservation agents were announcing the boarding zones. Shelton and Brandon looked at each other and smiled and said, "We are in First Class, baby." We all broke out in laughter.

When traveling across the pond, First Class is definitely the way to go. The seats are larger and softer, leg space is ridiculous, and the most important aspect to 16-year-old growing boys is the food. The food and drink in the front is plentiful and constant.

We boarded first. We all cracked up because of the looks we received by everyone passing. The looks probably ranged from "How in the world did they get up there?" to "Are they famous?" Inquiring minds wanted to know. Shelton tore into his First Class pack and pulled out his cool and comfy, red, First Class socks. The socks were thick and warm. Before long, Brandon said, "Mr. Sam, are we going to get to watch a movie?" I shook my head yes and he and Shelton gave each other some dap.

Both boys were ready for the trip of a lifetime. I made them both wear East Lake golf shirts and a pair of khaki pants. All of their clothing had been choreographed and pre-determined. They had sweaters, sweater vests, turtlenecks, long-sleeve shirts, no shorts, rain gear, and jackets. They were ready for the golf. They were ready for the elements. They were ready for their internship. They were ready for everything. At least I thought so. I was exhausted before we even took off. I had just left Atlanta five days prior for a slight vacay with my wife. We had flown to Kona, on the Big Island of Hawaii. The trip to Kona was planned for eight days, but I knew that I could only stay five. I know that you are thinking why not simply schedule the Hawaii trip at another time. This was the only opportunity that my wife could muster due to her work constraints. The only way to avoid any confusion with me leaving my wife alone in Hawaii, I paid for one of my cousins to fly in from Los Angeles. My cousin Debbie lived in Los Angeles and she was always excited to take a nice vacation. My wife really liked her and they would have the entire weekend in Kona to get massages, facials, and totally get pampered. By the way, everything was already paid in full.

After I landed in Atlanta from a long Hawaii trip, I had an eight-hour layover before having to pick up Shelton and Brandon. The Scotland trip would also be long, but memorable. I left the airport, went home to shower, and grabbed my bag that was already packed for the UK. After I ate a quick meal, I drove through East Lake and scooped up the boys. Now we were set! Four, three, two, one, takeoff! We were truly flying in the friendly skies.

The moment we landed in Edinburgh, we met Phil Sharpe. Phil is an unbelievable guy. Phil was born in Scotland but worked for PGA.com and lived in Atlanta.

Phil was like your favorite uncle. He told a lot of stories; he was funny and he was very kind and considerate.

The first thing we did was go to lunch. We had studied a lot of the British Open history; we talked about Bobby Jones and Charlie Yates and their victories across the pond. We had researched the weather. We had even researched a little history on the town of St. Andrews. But the one thing that we didn't focus on was the food. I had only mentioned to the boys that the Scots ate a lot of fish and chips.

The first meal might have been the defining moment. We stopped at a local tavern and Phil essentially ordered the local meal for the boys. Of course, the boys had the traditional fish and chips and then there was something else on the plate. It was called haggis. The boys looked at each other and started smiling and started digging in until Phil asked if they knew what they were eating. Shelton looked up with the haggis half hanging in his mouth. Brandon hadn't eaten it yet, but sensed something wasn't right with the dish. He burst out laughing. Shelton, embarrassed, said, "What is this, man?" The table erupted. Phil began to explain the origin of haggis. Haggis is a savory pudding containing sheep's pluck (heart, liver, and lungs) minced with onion, oatmeal, suet, spices, and salt, mixed with stock, and traditionally encased in the animal's stomach and simmered for approximately three hours. Most modern commercial haggis is prepared in a sausage casing rather than an actual stomach. Shelton almost threw up. We were laughing so hard that we began tearing up.

That was it. No more experiments. Pizza, fish, chips, and pop. From that moment on, the only thing they would eat would have to resemble American food. Imagine two boys from the "dirty South" with their southern twang, now add in some urban flair and popular slang, stir in a few words, and now top it off with a life-changing experience. This would be an exciting story and an incredible week. Their unique slang and Atlanta regional dialect along with their cultural inexperience made for a pay-per-view reality show. According to many in media, Atlanta has become the culture capital of America.

I am a big historian of the game. One of my old bosses at East Lake had given me a book about a father and his son enjoying time playing golf in Scotland. For any true student of the game, Scotland is the motherland of golf. It is the Mecca. It is the beginning and it definitely housed expanded roots.

I am an avid reader. I am a fan of anything golf related that I can get my hands on. I read magazines, periodicals, internet stories, and different types of golf books. Reading allows me to see golf through the lenses of the world. Before traveling to Bermuda, Scotland, Hawaii, Australia, China, Taiwan, Uganda, South Africa, the Caribbean, Canada, and Mexico and across the United States, I read about these places first in books and other publications.

The aforementioned book prompted me to create a trip with my dad over to Scotland. This experience with my dad made me exhaust all of my energy on the East Lake children. They didn't have fathers in the picture to play golf with nor was there anyone in the que to travel with. I knew that without some special intervention they would never make it across the pond. I am big on dreams. I have seen dreams come true on multiple occasions.

I had traveled to Scotland on several occasions. My most memorable trip was the two weeks spent with my dad. It was amazing. We were fortunate to play the Old Course. We were able to experience 90 holes of the most special golf that I had ever played in my life. From my experiences over there, I knew a trip with the boys would change their lives forever.

The Old Course at St. Andrews was the site of the 2005 British Open. I thought that if I could get a couple of the boys over there, it could potentially change the scope of opportunities for juniors throughout the junior golf network. I prayed and it worked. I broached the subject as an internship.

One of the members on my East Lake Junior Golf Academy Board held a key position at Turner Sports, which was in the TNT family. TNT had done a great job broadcasting the British Open in conjunction with the BBC. I tossed the idea at Drew Reifenberger in October 2004 and by March 2005 the trip was set in stone. Drew was a great guy.

Although he held a very influential position at the network, he hadn't been born with a silver spoon in his mouth. He was a visionary. He knew what the onset of hard work would and could do. He also realized that certain opportunities changed lives forever.

He told me on several occasions about things that he had done and learned while working that essentially set his career in motion. Drew also made sure that TNT picked up the lodging costs. The trip was setting up pretty nicely, but I knew the trip wouldn't happen without the plane tickets. I figured the only water we would cross without tickets would be the lake in the East Lake neighborhood, but I had faith. The funny part about all of this is that I was forced to navigate all of the internal channels in stealth mode. I had learned from experience that some projects would be automatically shot down unless certain execs came up with the ideas. I played the game. Everything I did was in the best interest of the children. My second home run brought the trip to fruition.

I called on my friend Scarlett Brown at Delta. I put together a simple proposal that gave Delta some recognition, which in turn gave us the tickets. Scarlett gave us First Class tickets to Manchester, England. We bought regular-fare tickets for the short flight from Manchester to Edinburgh, Scotland. If you have ever flown over to the United Kingdom, you know that the trip is a very long flight. The best class of seats allowed us to have larger seats, meals, movies, and, according to Brandon, the most comfortable red socks in the world. I had also worked through a few of my other contacts in order to set up some golf. We were able to play three rounds of golf in Scotland.

But the trip was indeed a learning experience. Shelton and Brandon served as runners or gophers for Ted Pio Roda, the TNT on-course photographer. The boys were taught how to use the photo editing software, and they were able to take the pictures and place them into the editing system. This was important for all of the TNT entities, which included PGA.com. The PGA.com professionals were able to access the photographs through the editing system and send them to all of the television and print partners, which included TNT, TBS, and the BBC. This was a vital cog in the wheel. The boys worked very diligently and closely with the PGA.com crew members, who served as their job supervisors. This allowed the boys to experience pressure in a real work environment. They played an important role in the production of the British Open.

We could actually say that we witnessed and participated in one of the most magical and historic weeks in the history of golf. While Shelton and Brandon were working, Tiger Woods was having an incredible four-day run of tournament golf. He concluded the week by winning the 2005 Open Championship. It was also the year when Jack Nicklaus played in his last Open Championship. We watched Jack walk across the famed bridge and play his final 18 holes at St. Andrews. I actually have a large picture of me and the boys on that same bridge hanging in my "man cave" in my house. The experience was truly amazing. The boys ate enough fish and chips to last a lifetime. It was also a unique experience from a cultural perspective. We were there for seven days and we were among only a handful of blacks at the Open Championship. An Australian woman walked up to me at the end of the week and said that she saw my sons everywhere during championship week. I laughed because I knew she meant well. She complimented them on their beautiful, striking physical features. I smiled and thanked her for her kind words. I guess the boys couldn't help but stick out. This is another example of why the game needs more diversity.

While walking across the 18th fairway at the conclusion of the practice round, David Toms and Stewart Cink stopped us and inquired about us being there. The boys had met them and played with them during the Tour Championship. Tom Lehman saw us and took the initiative to come over to talk to the boys. Tom had been very gracious. His generosity, but more importantly his kind heart, was always evident as it related to the kids.

During one of our trips to watch a practice round at the Masters, Tom saw us walking down the fairway on the 3rd hole. He actually walked inside and outside of the ropes while playing in order to chat with the boys. The boys had been fortunate enough to play with him during one of the first Tour Championships held at East Lake.

The Open Championship has a different feel. The players walk through the small towns for dinner. The spectators are able to walk on the fairways. The Open seems to embrace the common man.

The Scots have an unbelievable appreciation for the game of golf and most things associated with it. The experience was incredible.

CHAPTER 24

Winston Lake

"This is my commandment, That ye love one another,
as I have loved you."

(John 15:12)

I really loved my time in Atlanta. The experiences, the kids, the lessons, and the opportunities were awesome. When I sit back and reflect on "the Lake," I honestly think of another "Lake." My mind gravitates to Winston Lake Golf Course in Winston-Salem, North Carolina. This is the course where I grew up.

There were so many similarities between my upbringing and the life I was trying to carve out for the boys. The resemblances were scary. There was one guy who essentially served as the cynosure for a lot of black junior golfers in the mid- to late '70s. His name was Ernest Morris. Ernest was the assistant professional at Tanglewood Golf Course, which is on the outskirts of Winston-Salem. Tanglewood was about 20 minutes from my neighborhood. Ernest would drive into the neighborhood and pick up me and four of my buddies. I didn't know any better. He didn't pick us up for free, but he also didn't have to do it. We were always cramped in his small brown Chevrolet Chevette, but we never complained. Trust me… you never wanted to ride in the back seat. If you were the unfortunate soul who was forced to sit in the middle on the hump, you would be hurting for the rest of the day.

It was a brutal ride, but Ernest was always on time. Five days a week, Pro (we called Ernest "Pro") rode through the neighborhood and picked us up. He had committed his summers to teaching us golf. There was a small cadre of us who were really interested in the game. All of our dads played a lot of golf. In fact, all of our dads were really good golfers. Tanglewood did a lot for us. It was and still is the nicest park in Winston-Salem. It has horse riding stables, concerts, swimming pools, three golf courses, paddle boats, running and walking trails, and an incredible Christmas light display during the holidays. The group of juniors that assembled during the summers was huge and diverse. There were a handful of blacks in the program, but color never was an issue. We all had golf in common.

Ernest was later named the head golf professional at Winston Lake Golf Course. This is when my true golf maturation kicked in. It was only five minutes from the house and it was a tough track. The lessons learned on the range, the practice green, and the course were a given, but the things I learned from the other adults at the course on a daily basis would last a lifetime. Hitting balls on the driving range and studying in a classroom wouldn't have come close to the training I received from the old guys at the lake.

I learned about a dress code, passion for the game, gambling, course and game etiquette, respecting the game of life, opportunities, and mostly about the world. Most of the guys at the course seemed to have nicknames. Peter Pie, C'man, Art, Duck, Heavy, Pops, Popsy, Muhammad Herb, Hound, Gap, Shorty, Hiawatha, Vic Johnson, Crump, Shipman, Butch, Mr. Conrad, Ted, Harvey and Bobby, Lawyer Davis, Judge Al, Lil Jack, Eagle Eye, Pro, Red, Beaver, Lem, Fats, Tony C., Neal, and Iron Man were some of the regulars. For whatever it was worth, all of these guys served as extensions of my "real" family. I learned so much from the golf course. I learned what to do but more importantly what *not* to do. I learned not to be a womanizer or an abuser, learned not to do drugs and I learned that hard work was the only true path to economic freedom.

There were also some scandalous ass things that went on at the course.

First case in point: My dad and my Uncle Earl had teamed up against a couple of course regulars on this particular Tuesday. Muscle Neck and Tubs were the chosen two on this beautifully sunny day. My dad and uncle were four holes up heading into the 10th hole. This was a big-money game. They were gambling, playing the normal game of rabbit and squirrel for $10 each, which also included all birdies paying out at $25. The winner of each nine holes also received $20 with the clinch. You could win a leg on a rabbit by simply winning the hole, but you had to win the hole making a birdie in order to win a leg on the squirrel. This was always a competitive way to compete because it gave all four participants a chance.

By the time my dad and uncle made the turn, they were up $250. Tubs leaned over and gave his partner a fist bump and walked up to my dad and said, "Hey, give me about 15 minutes. I need to run up to the bank to get some extra cash to cover our bets." He continued, "Can I borrow your car, Sam, because my girlfriend dropped me off." My dad didn't think too much and let him use our 1956 doodoo-brown Buick Roadmaster. My dad and uncle joked at the drubbing that they were giving Tubs and Muscle Neck as they proceeded into the clubhouse.

The food inside was decent, but the clubhouse grill was famous for its classic ham and cheese sandwiches. These sandwiches were amazing. You would get them out of a fridge and place them in a rotating oven. They were buttery toasted and ridiculously tasty. I have probably eaten about 250 of them in my lifetime. In all transparency, the sandwiches were the real reason why I followed my father out to the course in the first place when I was a little boy. He would always give me a handful of money, which was typically about $5. I would use the money to buy three of the sandwiches and I would always drink a large Tahitian Treat.

After about 15 minutes, Tubs returned with a brown paper sack and the golf round continued. Tubs paid off his front nine bets and then got crazy and doubled the bets on the back side. My dad and my uncle cleaned up. They beat the brakes off these guys. At the end of the match, they had won $320 respectively. This extra cash would make my mom happy, since this would serve as rent money.

On the way home, while sitting in the back seat, I started to tease my dad and uncle, saying they were financially starving my mom and my aunt. I was asking them about the money stashed under the seat and the money stuck in the crevices between the seats. Since my dad was driving, my uncle turned around and said, "What the hell are you talking about?" Uncle Earl was hilarious. He spoke a few languages and they would come out at the most random of times. During the quick examination, he looked at my dad and said in German, "You ain't gonna believe this shit." There were $50 bills and $100 bills literally stuffed in the cracks of the seats. There were also a ton of empty money wrappers thrown about the back seat. The car grew quiet.

Later that evening, my parents were watching the news and a segment came on about a local bank robbery in East Winston. It mentioned that the Wachovia Bank had been robbed at 2:35 p.m. earlier that day by a black guy with a R. J. Reynolds golf hat on. Quizzically I looked at my dad and he looked at me and he simply walked out of the room. It was pretty easy to connect the dots.

Tubs was a really big, scary-looking dude. He was only about six-two, but he was a grizzly-shaped 260 pounds. Most of the old men at the course made it their mission to never cross him. They were afraid of him. We all knew he carried a gun in his golf bag. He had served a lot of time in prison and his family had a very reckless reputation. The weirdest thing was that he was really nice to me and he really liked my dad. I surmised that after making the turn while down $250, he borrowed my dad's car and subsequently robbed the local Wachovia Bank. My dad and I never spoke about that day again. I definitely didn't want my dad to come back in a body bag.

Many years later, Tubs was killed in New Jersey. He and his buddy were driving to New York City and during a routine traffic stop on the New Jersey Turnpike, Tubs got pissed at the trooper's attitude and reached for his gun. The trooper reacted too quickly and he shot and killed Tubs at the scene. Tubs didn't have a conscience and, in the end, it cost him his life. My dad always told me that nothing good could ever come out of gambling. I knew then that gambling was truly a dead end. The next day when I got in the car to ride to the course all of the bills were gone. I never said another word about the buffoonery from the previous day.

This wasn't the only crazy scenario that I witnessed at the "Lake."

On a very hot and humid summer day, Buck and Beaver were coming off the 18th green. Beaver was about five-foot-eight and 260 pounds while Buck was six-foot-two and 190 pounds soaking wet. Beaver owned his own construction company and Buck drove a city bus. They parked their carts up in front of the old clubhouse. The other two guys in the foursome, Duck and C'Man, started pulling out their wallets so that they could settle their bets. Everything seemed to be going smoothly. Out of the corner of my right eye, I saw Buck hand Beaver a fat wad of cash. This normally suffices to consummate the round, but this is when the "real" round started. Buck and Beaver began arguing rather vehemently about what I thought was the bet. Although Buck was handing the cash over, he was becoming incensed and undone. After a little back and forth, Beaver stuck his chest out, grabbed a 9-iron, and took a mighty swing at Buck's head. He missed!

Buck scrambled over to his large Ping staff bag, reached into the ball pocket, and pulled out a .22-caliber handgun. As Buck raised the gun to pop a cap into Beaver, Lil Jack tackled him. Beaver turned and made a mad dash down the hill into the parking lot. Lil Jack and about five other guys held onto Buck until he calmed down. Crazy! What's crazier is that the police were never called.

After a few weeks of hanging around the course, I found out the true origin of the ruckus. Buck had been secretly sleeping with Beaver's wife. I guess Beaver figured that it was bad enough having his wife step out on him with Buck, but losing money to him on the golf course made the situation unbearable. About 20 years later after teeing off on the 520-yard, par-5 3rd hole, Duck Downs teed off with his 3-wood and retreated to the cart, preparing to drive to his second shot. After placing his 3-wood in his golf bag, he sat on the golf cart and died. God didn't even allow him to finish the hole. His life literally left his body like a high, soft, butter fade on a dogleg right. He was an incredibly nice old man. He was super kind to me. This was my upbringing in East Winston. I loved it all and I wouldn't have traded any of it for anything in the world.

CHAPTER 25

Lessons Learned

"As for the one who is weak in faith, welcome him, but not to quarrel over opinions. One person believes he may eat anything, while the weak person eats only vegetables. Let not the one who eats despise the one who abstains, and let not the one who abstains pass judgment on the one who eats, for God has welcomed him. Who are you to pass judgment on the servant of another? It is before his own master that he stands or falls. And he will be upheld, for the Lord is able to make him stand. One person esteems one day as better than another, while another esteems all days alike. Each one should be fully convinced in his own mind."

(Romans: 14:1-23)

I learned how to gamble. I am not proud of it, but I learned the universal language of playing for rabbits and squirrels. I was never allowed to bet with the old dudes, but I learned the trade. These guys were very protective of "Little Sam" and they didn't let me play in their money games. They never realized that my being around the game really made me super curious. One day I tried to put everything that I'd learned into play and it temporarily cost me the game that I loved.

When I was 10 years old, I had taken a road trip down to Duke University with the tournament traveling team from my golf course. We were playing against some statewide juniors. Once we jumped out of the car, we all ran to the putting green and waited for Ernest to sign us in before our tee time. While we were waiting, one of the white kids named Grant and I agreed to play a little "game." The game consisted of targeted putts, which cost 10 cents apiece. After putting for a while, I had run his tab up to a $1.00. Grant decided to quit playing since he was already down a buck. He started to get on my nerves with his comments. It was also bothering me that he was balking on the bet. Grant was acting pretty entitled and arrogant. We had a few words and without thinking, I hit him in the mouth. I figured the punch would get his attention and shut him up.

The only thing on my mind was my money. This is probably why I constantly preached to the juniors that betting is for the birds. Betting is not very beneficial in the big scheme of things. I probably shouldn't have interjected my baggage on the boys, but I figured there had to be easier ways to make a few bucks. I never explained to them why, but I definitely had my reason. Ernest came out of the clubhouse and realized what had just transpired and he blew a gasket. He was livid. He put me in his little "brown hornet" (nickname we gave his brown Chevette) and hurriedly drove me the two hours back to Winston-Salem. He banned me from the golf course and said I wasn't allowed to play until he said so, which might stretch throughout the entire summer.

I had grown up with Ernest. Ernest was six feet tall and about 210 pounds. He had a slight Coors light belly and big, strong forearms. He always dressed nice with his crisply pressed golf shirts and creased slacks. He had an incredible assortment of Dexter golf shoes. He always told people that I introduced him to his wife. Many years earlier while making the normal morning trek to Tanglewood Golf Course during the summers, Ernest would always get an errand or two in. He loved to visit the First Union Bank and he only utilized the drive-thru. I also liked going to the bank with Ernest because he always got me a couple of suckers from the pretty lady in the window. The teller kept a huge cup of suckers in the window and she was definitely generous with them.

He drew up the nerve to introduce himself to the teller and increase the depth of their conversations. One thing led to another and Ernest eventually married her. Her name was Gwen and she was a super-nice lady. I kind of figured he was sweet on her, but I thought she was amazing because of the candy. Ernest and I had a great relationship. I took some things for granted, but I was always respectful. I viewed him more of an uncle instead of a boss. As I aged, I thought I would automatically accrue playing privileges, but Ernest made sure it didn't work that way. My parents had always emphasized the belief that people don't get something for nothing. My parents were correct. A lot of what I deemed I learned from Ernest at the course had actually been initiated at home. They just seemed to make more sense coming from someone else. The rhetoric was repetitive, but effective.

He made me earn all of my practice and playing privileges. When he offered me the job working at Winston Lake, I thought money was going to be involved. I was 13 years old and I couldn't wait to get paid, but he had other ideas. There would be no pay. He made me vacuum the clubhouse, empty trash, sweep up cigarette butts outside, and do anything else that needed to be done. I didn't understand it then, but it all made sense once I started running the East Lake program.

I constantly stayed on the boys in East Lake about their appearance and their level of respect and accountability for their surroundings. This wasn't an accident. This is how life had been presented to me. I saw myself in so many of them. I was a lot like the boys. I always tried to wear my favorite pair of Adidas sweatpants along with my high school golf shirt to the golf course.

Although my parents had stocked my closet with an overkill of golf clothes, I had developed my favorites. The problem with my outfit was simple. I wore it when I painted, cleaned golf carts, and played golf. Don't get me wrong, I washed the clothes all the time, but I wasn't unlike many golfers on tour at the time. I had read that a lot of golfers on tour had favorite outfits. Some thought certain shirts and pants helped them fare better during their competitions. I felt the same way. The pants had paint on them that would never wash off. The pants also had a hole in the crotch. I always thought it kept the air flowing in all the right places. In hindsight I now know that dressing like this was absurd.

I guess one day Pro had simply had enough. He called me in his office and laid down the law. He asked me if I owned any other outfits. He definitely knew the answer! Ernest was trying to be funny because he lived down the street from my family in Ebony Hills. He knew how we were living. He was trying to prove a point. He told me that I could no longer play golf or work in the Adidas pants or the old golf shirt. He wasn't smiling. He was serious. He went on to talk about how successful people dressed and the importance of appearance. He used the analogy of my dad wearing a suit every day to work as an example. I got the drift. My dad wore a suit and tie to the job every day. He was always clean and professional. It was the way he had been trained. I kept my mouth shut and followed the plan. I retired the raggedy golf clothes and promised to do better. The outfit was history. I threw the pants and shirt away later that evening. I respected him like family and I knew that he was helping to prepare me for something later in life.

I was taught early and often during my formative years the difference between right and wrong. I loved to play golf. I had figured out a shortcut or an easier way to play a loop of seven or eight holes. These holes allowed me an expedited round and also allowed me to stay out of everyone's way. I thought I had it figured out. One evening while trying to beat the clock, I was trying to squeeze in as many holes as I could before the sun went down. After finishing the 9th hole, I played down hole No. 1 and played up the 18th hole. I jumped across to the 12th hole because I was intending on finishing on the 18th hole again. Before teeing off on the 17th hole, I actually looked around for approaching groups. I didn't see a soul. I teed it up on the 18th and slapped a drive down the right side in the rough close to the tree line.

While looking for my ball in the rough, I heard a golf ball land in the fairway about 10 yards to the right of me. I had never been hit by a golf shot, but I had seen a few folks get hit. I didn't want today to be my turn in the rotation. The sound of the second ball forced me to run and hide behind a tree. I heard the third ball hit in the rough and I watched it roll about 30 feet ahead of me. I was thinking there was absolutely no way I could get hit hiding behind a tree. I heard the fourth crack of the club and I actually saw it land on the left side on the fairway close to the rough, but the weirdest thing happened. The ball hit the ground and immediately changed directions and made a severe right-angle turn, which was directly toward me. This startled the shit out of me. I froze! The ball sought me out like a heat-seeking missile as it knocked the hell out of my leg. I was pissed. Without thinking and without much care, I irresponsibly picked up the ball and teed it up in the center of the fairway. I was about to get retribution. My goal was to hit one of the guys back on the tee box.

At this point in my golf development, my tee game was the strongest part of the game. I played a low-flighted stinger aimed directly at the tee box. The shot was incredibly accurate. The ball split the guys on the tee. They immediately jumped on the cart and headed in my direction. I saw them coming and I grabbed my clubs and ran as fast as I could to the clubhouse because I knew that "it was about to go down." I had already made up my mind that I was probably going to have to lay "some hands" on somebody. I knew I was wrong for jumping in front of the guys, but I didn't think they should have hit me. I was young, naive, and very stubborn. I was only 16 years old, but definitely old enough to know better. I was in the wrong, but I didn't have time to process it at this moment.

The guys were Canadian. They caught me at the clubhouse and they were irate. Ernest came outside when he heard all the commotion. After the Canadians explained their story, Pro looked at me. He was pissed. When I think back on it, I think he probably wanted to choke me. I was trying to explain my side of the story, but when you are playing for free, you don't really have a side of the story, especially when you were wrong anyway for jumping holes and playing the course out of sequence. Ernest apologized to the guys and bought them a drink. In fact, he must have done a good job, because the Canadians wanted to know more about my plight playing junior golf rather than them being upset with me. Controlling your emotions on the golf course became a common theme for me during my junior golf years.

I was out playing by myself one day and I found a really nice beryllium copper Cleveland wedge on the course. The Cleveland wedges were the chic new specialty clubs in golf and I didn't have one. I never liked to ask my parents to buy me anything. I am sure they would have bought me one if I had asked, but I didn't ask. On the way up to the clubhouse, I stopped by the range. I wanted to hit about 20 or 30 shots with the newfound wedge. Although I would have loved to keep the club, I knew better. I believed in Karma. I had always heard that good things happened to good people. I had definitely been taught and trained to be honest. I was taught that my integrity was in many cases more important than my name.

I went into the pro shop and gave Ernest the wedge. I mentioned that I had taken it to the range and hit a few shots with it. A couple of days later upon my arrival at the course, Ernest walked up to me and handed me a club. It was a Cleveland wedge. In fact, it was the same wedge that I had found on the course a couple of days earlier. I said, "What are you doing?" He said that the guy who had lost the club came back later that day to retrieve it. He asked Ernest who had found the club. He pointed to me down on the range. He asked Pro about my golf handicap. Ernest told him and also told him that I had several colleges and universities offering me golf scholarships. He told Pro to keep the wedge and he wanted me to have it. He wished me luck. I never found out the guy's name, but this act of kindness was huge in my personal development. As a side note, I used the wedge throughout college and I still have it in my garage to this day.

One of my favorite pastimes was retreating to the driving range to watch golf shots. I loved to watch the old black men hit balls. This was also the place where they told the most lies about their golf games. Watching their swings was like reading poetry. Some swings were written in Trochaic meter and some in iambic meter. They weren't pretty or technically sound, but they were all effective. Everyone had a different swing. Some of their swings were dictated by their big stomachs, some were dictated by the cigars or cigarettes in their mouths, and some were dictated by their physical disposition. But the one thing most of the old cats did while they practiced was talk. They talked all the damn time.

One of my favorite people was a guy named C'Man. He was great to talk to. They called him C'Man because he always played a little cut shot (fade) on the course. (A cut shot for a right-handed player is a ball traveling from left to right.) He always wore a kangol hat and he always had a cigarette in the corner of his mouth. When he would talk, the cigarette would be bouncing up and down like a basketball. I think C'Man looked at me as the person I was capable of becoming. He totally respected my dad. He would always tell me to obey my parents and never to take them for granted. He opened up and talked to me a lot about drugs.

One day out of the blue, he opened up and started to expose me to his earlier life. He told me to stay away from drugs because he had experienced them and he had been a heavy user. He told me that he had been a heroin addict. He also delved into how it affected his life. He talked about his journey of cleaning up his life. He said his life had totally taken a 360-degree turn for the best. He was focused on doing things the right way now. I really respected him. I never judged him. C'Man didn't live too far from us. When I would ride my bike over to my friend's house, I would always stop by to talk to him. C'Man was one of the realest people I knew. I never knew why he opened up to me, but when I got older, I constantly thanked him. God places people in our lives for a variety of reasons. I didn't question the process. I just tried to remain humble and gracious. There is a great verse in Colossians 2:6-7 that reads, "So then, just as you received Christ Jesus as Lord, continue to live your lives in him, strengthened in the faith, as you were taught, and overflowing with thankfulness."

These scenarios are only a few examples of the myriad lessons that I learned at the golf course. Fittingly, these were the same lessons that I was trying to instill into the Atlanta youth. Experience has always been one of the best teachers. A lot of the guys who carried the great nicknames are now deceased. Their lessons live in me, but now they also abide within the children of the East Lake neighborhood. There is a C'Man or an Ernest in all our lives. I was the Ernest to the children in East Lake. My goal for them was that they grow up to serve the same role in someone else's life one day.

CHAPTER 26

Drop It Like It's Hot

"Finally, all of you, have unity of mind, sympathy, brotherly love, a tender heart, and a humble mind."

(1 Peter 3:8)

The mission of the East Lake Junior Golf Academy was to create a safe haven for the children in the local community. I continually pushed the program's top brass. Many felt the community should focus solely on serving the youth who lived in the 30317 zip code. I thought creating an inclusive program would benefit everyone down the road. I thought working with and nurturing the neighborhood children was great, but I thought opening the program to outsiders would assist the neighborhood children and serve as a home run for the community.

I was amazed at some of the closed-door discussions. There were times when I felt many of those in charge, who happened to be white, thought about this neighborhood like a scientist thinks about amoebas in a Petri dish. I used to laugh internally at how some of the folks treated the residents of the community like dangling puppets. They knew what type of education was best, and they knew about the best types of recreational options to have in the neighborhood. They also thought they knew which sports were best to offer at the school, and they definitely thought they knew what was best for "black kids."

For the record, I am black. This is to serve as no disrespect, but I had been around other black children all my life. I had also been around whites and other nationalities. I think we all benefitted from growing up around children who were different. I learned early that all children benefit when rich children play with poor children and nationalities mix. I fought the exclusion piece with East Lake. I will give them credit because after several years of pressing the issue, they sort of relented. In other words, they worked with me and supported the program since we were experiencing success developing the youth.

One afternoon while sitting in my office, I got a phone call. The voice on the other end had a strong accent with a pure scent of innocence. He introduced himself as Mihkel Nurm. Mihkel was 14 years old and he was from a place called Estonia, a Northern European country next door to Russia.

Estonia is a country on the eastern coast of the Baltic Sea in Northern Europe. It is bordered to the north by the Gulf of Finland with Finland on the other side, to the west by the Baltic Sea with Sweden on the other side, to the south by Latvia, and to the east by Lake Peipus and Russia.

Its capital and largest city is Tallinn, with a population of 1.3 million. Mihkel was from Tallinn.

While he was telling me about his homeland, all I could think about was their weather. I was imagining him standing on a slightly elevated range hitting golf balls in the midst of snow drifts. The elevation would allow the hitting area to not develop an accumulation.

In the neighborhood we called Mihkel "Michael." He told me that his mother was in a doctorate program over at Emory University in Atlanta and that he really loved golf. He wanted to know if he could come over and practice with us. I told him to come over in order for me to watch his swing. My thought process was simple. We were already working with 1,000 children a year and a lot of those children had some really funky golf swings. But more importantly, a lot of those children didn't even want to be there. Because of our relationships with different entities, including the charter school and the YMCA, the children were forced to come to golf. I am glad that we forced them. I think children need help in making positive choices in the beginning. It's like the child saying they don't like vegetables and yet they have never tried them.

Sure enough Mihkel, his little sister, and their mother showed up at the golf course the next day. They were a true delight. Mihkel was a short, stocky fellow with a military haircut and a lot of will. His mother seemed really nice. While we stood on the range, I watched Mihkel hit about 50 to 100 balls and gave him "my" speech. To me the most important part of being good at anything is the dedication, desire, and passion related to the craft. I told the family that the most important part of our relationship was going to be transparency, trust, and effort. I told them that as long as Mihkel showed up on time and was willing to assist some of the younger kids, he would always be welcomed.

It was a great relationship. He showed up in the rain, sleet, or sunshine. The temperature was never an issue. He wanted it bad. He was a straight-A student in school, spoke four languages, and was very proficient in math. Mihkel did everything I asked him to do. The best golfers in the program began to take notice of Mihkel's work ethic and eventually they quietly grew fond of him. They definitely wanted to know more about him and his origins.

I subtlety forced all the kids to talk and interact by pairing them together on the course. Mihkel was not as good as my best golfers, but he listened intently to me on the range. He lived on every word of instruction. This was great because for some time I had noticed my regulars beginning to take the game for granted. They had experienced a little success and were genuinely getting the "big head." They didn't think they needed regular instruction, yet they always got pissed when they didn't do well in tournaments.

This was always an interesting phenomenon. These children initially played and practiced with a purpose. They had been groomed to compete with each other. Their world was very restricted. A few of my regulars had vaulted to the top of the neighborhood pecking order.

The figurative pecking order with Mihkel was different. I think they felt a little threatened. Mihkel's game improved by leaps and bounds. In the first few months, his handicap dropped from a 16 to a solid 7. The neighborhood boys started observing his practice habits. I would tell the regulars that Mihkel was going to catch them and they would always laugh and tell me to "stop trippin.'" They paid attention and watched with regularity. When Mihkel showed up, the neighborhood boys automatically headed up to the range. It appeared as though they didn't want to be outdone.

Mihkel was consistent and persistent. The neighborhood boys stopped complaining about the inclement weather and started to challenge the conditions. The culture had shifted. After months of this, it seemed as if the light finally came on. The neighborhood boys totally opened up. I had purposely included Mihkel in all our activities. They benefitted from a child who spoke four languages and a child making straight As in school.

My experiment worked. I took Mihkel to his first professional sporting event with the neighborhood kids. We went to see the Atlanta Hawks play. This kid must have asked me a million questions about the basketball game. In his words, he had never seen men up close who were so large. This was a unique social experiment that would pay dividends in my recruitment prowess many years later when I became a collegiate coach.

Mihkel impacted all of our lives, but we also made a lasting impression on him. During this time in pop culture in Atlanta, the neighborhood kids listened to the major rap and hip-hop radio station Hot 97.5 FM. The kids swore by the station. One day while walking up to the range, I saw the boys letting Mihkel listen to "their" music. He was being introduced to "their" station. The rap industry had literally exploded in Atlanta during the early 2000s. Atlanta had become a hub for a lot of aspiring talent: Ludacris, Ying Yang Twins, Goodie Mob, Outkast, Andre 3000, Young Joc, T.I., and Shawty Lo (whose son was in my program). Many more were arriving on the music scene with abandon.

One day Mihkel walked up to me and said, with his strong accent, "Mr. Sam, drop it like it's hot." I laughed because this was the slogan from the station. The station had gained a new fan.

Mihkel's impact was huge on the program on so many levels. The level of discipline, attention to detail, increased practice time, and a more detailed attention to academics had intensified. Mihkel benefitted from the neighborhood boys' level of play. He was determined to beat them, and one day all of the lessons and pressure came to a head.

On a very cold afternoon in the ATL, I sent all the boys out to play. They were qualifying for spots. I was going to take the top four golfers to play in a local match against some really advanced juniors. It was about 40 degrees, but tensions were getting heated. After the first six holes, Mihkel was down by five strokes to the other boys. His face showed frustration and befuddlement. I was watching from the 4th green. After Mihkel putted out on the 6th green, he picked up his ball and headed up the hill to the range. The other boys continued and headed off to the 7th tee box. I watched him get two buckets of balls and I approached him in a state of disbelief.

I said, "Why did you stop playing? You still have a lot of holes left and although you didn't start off well, you can catch the boys."

He said, "Mr. Sam I am not playing well. I wanted to come up here and work on my swing."

I listened intently. After a brief respite, I asked him to get his cell phone and call his mother. He gave me a quizzical look and I continued. I said please call your mother because she needs to come and pick you up. He asked why. I told him this was probably the last day that I would allow him to be a part of the program. He called his mother and I allowed him to hit balls until she came. When his mother arrived, I sat them both down and gave them my stance.

This is what I told them. The program that I was building at East Lake was more about building great people and not just about developing great golfers. I told them that I didn't believe in quitters. If he was quitting now in a competition because of a poor start, he was setting himself up to quit in life. I told them that I was treating Mihkel like everyone else. All of the regulars knew if they quit during a competition, then they were done. They knew where I stood and they also knew I would make it really tough on them in order to earn their way back in my good graces.

Mihkel was dumbfounded. He apologized and teared up. He told me he was mad at himself for not beating any of the guys and he thought hitting more balls would prepare him for the next opportunity. He continued to apologize and he and his mother reiterated that he would never quit again. I accepted his apology and told him this was the last time we would have this conversation.

That conversation did wonders for the program. Although the boys knew that I had kept children from participating because of behavior and discipline, they had never seen me threaten to take the "game" away. They were also the beneficiaries of Mihkel's action. I never had another issue like that again. Mihkel weathered the proverbial storm. He always showed up in a short-sleeve shirt. He came early and he was always the last person on the range. He stayed with the program for two years. He and his family left when his mother completed her doctoral program and they went back to Estonia. We missed him when he left, and I always hoped to remain in contact with him in the future.

We are in touch to this day via social media, and I think his introduction into the lives of the neighborhood boys was special. He and the boys developed great relationships. Years later on one of my trips to Scotland with Brandon and Shelton, we discovered Mihkel was there competing in a junior competition representing his country.

Mihkel is just one story, but the city of Atlanta was full of so many wonderful stories. I think all programs should open their program doors to some extent. The doors allow people in, but they also allow stories to be created. A clenched fist can't reach and help anyone get up. I realize that the financial implications and staffing components will always be major issues for programs around the country, but the innate lessons learned will stay with these children for a lifetime.

CHAPTER 27

Jail School

"The Spirit of the Lord is upon me, because he hath
anointed me to preach the gospel to the poor; he hath
sent me to heal the brokenhearted, to preach deliverance
to the captives, and recovering of sight to the blind,
to set at liberty them that are bruised."

(Luke 4:18)

There was an old school in the neighborhood, before the foundation tore it down and built a new one, that was scary. The school didn't have any windows, but more importantly, the only children who attended the school lived right there in the "projects." This set-up was comparable to jail and prison. I have always wondered how convicts can totally be rehabbed when they spend their entire day around other locked-up inmates. Many of these inmates could care less about life. How can a surgeon learn about surgery if he spends 100 percent of his time around people who dig ditches or play sports?

I think diversity is good in every situation. I have always thought that we can all learn from each other. The neighborhood was also full of residents who shared the same socio-economic ilk. If I want to get off food stamps or government assistance, do I ask my neighbor who is in the same boat for help? Wouldn't it be more beneficial to ask a neighbor who has a great job who isn't in the system for some advice?

The socio-economic petri dish was working in East Lake, as it related to housing, but not the junior golf program. The mixed-income housing philosophy really helped change the local perspectives on the financial wherewithal in the community. These thoughts seemed pure. Since the neighborhood property values were increasing and new houses were coming online, the diversity of residents would naturally take place. This indeed did happen. Most of the people moving into the neighborhood were white, and they were the only ones who could afford the half-million-dollar and up homes. They were initially placing their children in private schools, but now the tide had turned and these children were now attending the neighborhood Drew Charter School.

Drew Charter has been incredibly successful reaching these students. During the spring of 2014, the East Lake Foundation built the most impressive high school that I have ever seen. It came at a cost of $75 million, but it has already proven to be worthy of the investment. The neighborhood will now be able to work with a young person in kindergarten and follow them all the way through their high school graduation. The kindergarten through eighth grade model, which opened in 2000, set the tone for an impressive explosion of positive academics. The formative years will be cemented with proper fundamentals. The original Charles Drew elementary school, which was built before the neighborhood revitalization, didn't have any windows. The new school in the community is completely constructed with only windows. There is a window panel covering every inch of the new high school.

Experience has shown me that there are huge advantages when we place different types of people together. This model truly works. During the 2019 Georgia State High School Golf Championships, Charles R. Drew Charter High School made history by becoming the first team from APS to win a state golf championship. Drew's golf team also became the first all-African American team to win a state championship in the state of Georgia.

CHAPTER 28

Today

"And out of the ground made the Lord God to grow
every tree that is pleasant to the sight, and good for food;
the tree of life also in the midst of the garden, and the
tree of knowledge of good and evil."

(Genesis 2:9)

I have endured an incredible journey. My faith and my belief in God has carried me down some very exciting but complex roads. I have carved out a unique niche for myself. The administrations at Stanford, Michigan State, and Queens University all knew that one of my strongest gifts in coaching was recognizing and recruiting talent. I turned this into a business. Today I am the president of Pure Swings Golf Solutions, LLC (www.puryeargolf.com). My company conducts Nike Camps and places juniors from around the world in American universities and colleges in order to play golf. We conduct motivational speaking for corporations, and we evaluate golfers throughout various parts of the world.

My ability and opportunity to work with the young people in the East Lake neighborhood was indeed transformative. It served as a springboard for me. I assessed talent, motivated young people from a variety of backgrounds, and taught young people to trust their instincts. I have been able to maintain a national voice as a prominent spokesperson for minority golf in the country. My efforts have garnered recognition from CNN, ESPN, Disney Channel, *Inside the PGA*, Big Ten Network, and other media outlets.

After a lot of soul searching and a lot of prayer, I left the East Lake Junior Golf Academy at the end of 2005 and jumped into the collegiate coaching ranks as the first full-time men's assistant golf coach at Stanford University. During my stay on the West Coast, the Cardinal won the 2007 NCAA Division I national championship.

I never in my wildest dreams ever considered getting into the collegiate coaching ranks. In fact, I enjoyed it from the 20,000-foot view. I was like the coach in the coaching box at the top of the stadium. My brother definitely deserves a ton of credit here. Eric was a collegiate football coach out at Southwest Baptist University in Missouri. He was doing really well. We talked a lot about coaching philosophies and coaching schematics. We always discussed procedures and process. We constantly discussed the team's preparation and also his attention to details.

He is a brilliant dude. There was a reason that the Naval Academy recruited him to play football out of high school. He deserves a major shout-out. During one of our conversations, he referenced meeting the golf coaches at his university. He was like, man, you would be an incredible collegiate golf coach. This was a new concept to me. He continued. He said my budget running the program at East Lake was much larger than most collegiate golf budgets. He said I definitely knew the game and I knew how to teach it. He said the key would be motivation and my ability to reach the students. In most instances, he said, "you are reaching them where they are at that given time."

All of this verbiage was surprising and interesting. My brother had spent a lot of time around my East Lake Junior Golf Academy students both on and off the golf course. He also knew their environment, their upbringing, and definitely their golfing abilities.

This conversation really intrigued me. I started doing my research on collegiate programs. Outside of taking students to collegiate golf camps, my only experience dealing with collegiate programs was through my time playing collegiately at Tennessee State University. After doing my due diligence, I realized that my brother was correct.

I know that I say this a lot, but I truly believe that all of our steps are ordered by God. My brother gave me a website to search. The truth of the matter is I honestly forgot about the website and the coaching dream for months. I viewed it only as knowledge.

Then one day during my lunch break at the course, I decided to get on the computer and go to the website. I saw an opportunity for an assistant coaching position at Stanford University. I had never visited the campus, but I was well aware of Stanford's storied history. Tiger and Tom Watson played at Stanford. Watson was my favorite golfer growing up. Something went through me internally and I picked up the phone and called my wife. I said, "Hey, guess what…I just identified my next golf job."

She laughed. She said, "Have you been applying for jobs?"

I said, "No."

She continued, "So who is the company and where are they located?"

I was on the other end of the phone laughing. I said, "The job is in California at Stanford University."

She blurted out, "California!"

I said, "Yes."

She said, "I am not moving to California."

I responded, "I knew that would be your response." I kept going. I said, "When I get the job, we can place money in an account and we can fly to see each other twice a month." We laughed out loud, but at that point, my position was set. My gut and my prayers had told me that the opportunity out at Stanford would be a great fit.

I shared this story with one of my buddies at the course. He and I had become very close. Although he was a local executive at one of the large Fortune 500 companies in Atlanta, he was one of my best volunteers. I knew Rocky really cared about the kids. He was a terrific golfer, but he was a better person. During the conversation, he told me that he would hate to lose me in Atlanta, but that he would love to have me out on the "Farm." The "Farm" is the name associated with the Stanford campus out in Palo Alto. He said, "Sam did you forget that I played golf at Stanford?" In fact, I had forgotten, but I appreciated him reminding me. I shared with Rocky that I had applied for the position. Instead of him being skeptical or dismissive, he was incredibly encouraging and helpful. One thing led to another and the move to Cali was history. I was blessed to receive the opportunity. I used it to influence lives, but now on a much different canvas.

Once on the Farm, a lot of my creativity and ability working with youth was on display almost instantly. After we completed the 2005-06 season, I had an idea. We had talent, but we were missing the mental component, which stemmed from a winning culture. Stanford had won a lot over the years, but the Cardinal had experienced a national championship drought. The kids were very bright, but holistically, the "dog or killer" seemed to be missing from a few of the players. When Tiger, Casey, Notah, Christian Cevaer, Steve Burdick, Jim Seki, and Will Yanagisawa played on the "Farm," competing teams realized that they were probably playing for second place. The Stanford teams in the early 1990s were dynamic. I approached Conrad Ray, the head coach and also a player for the Cardinal during some of the glory years, and mentioned that I wanted to bring in a group from Atlanta to work on the team's mental approach for the upcoming season. Shawn Huff, a personal friend, led this group. Shawn did an excellent job carving out and crafting a mental toughness approach for our team through a bevy of leadership principles. The timing was perfect and the ideals were set.

CHAPTER 29

New Beginnings

"Bear with each other and forgive one another
if any of you has a grievance against someone.
Forgive as the Lord forgave you."

(Colossians 3:13)

We had recruited and brought in two of the best juniors in the country, Joseph Bramlett (who is currently playing on the PGA Tour) and Jordan Cox. We also had some incredible upperclassmen. The seminar set the tone and the pace for what would follow. The culture of the team improved. Conrad told me that if we did our jobs as coaches, we should be able to win it big by our fifth year. I corrected him. I promised Conrad that if he let me do what I knew how to do well, which was work with young people, that we could potentially win in two. This was the beginning of year two for us.

Conrad had taken a chance on me and I had owed him my best. I had become the first black assistant golf coach in the Pac-10. I had become the first assistant golf coach at Stanford. I always prided myself in playing to my strengths and not my weaknesses. The experiment worked. We won seven tournaments during the 2006-07 season with an average individual score of 69.80. It had been four years since the Cardinal had won a tournament. We concluded the season with three players winning individual titles and five players being selected All-Americans. The year culminated with a national championship victory and a trip to the White House to meet George W. Bush.

Three of the older leaders of the team during the 2006-07 season were Zack Miller, Matt Savage, and Rob Grube. These guys were great in the classroom, but just as special on the golf course. They were recognized as All-Americans by the GCAA, along with one of the freshman, Joseph Bramlett. Grube and Miller also recorded multiple individual tournament wins during this national championship season. By the way, Grube is only one of two four-year All Americans to ever come out of the university. Zack saw the future writing on the wall heading into the championship season.

"My thoughts heading into the season were very granular and not very groundbreaking. I was already battling it out with Rob and there was no chance I was going to let the top two high school recruits beat me. I changed my putter and wanted to be better and have great finishes," Miller said.

"I was excited heading into my senior season," Savage said. "The prior years were great learning experiences and we wanted to make it a great year."

During my handshake with the president, he definitely made sure to tell me that Dr. Condoleezza Rice (secretary of state) on his staff played a lot of golf and she was very good at it. Many years later I would be fortunate enough to host Dr. Rice for a round of golf in Charlotte.

Interestingly enough, if times nationally had been as perverse as they are now with our current national leadership, I am not sure the team would have elected to go to Washington after winning the national championship. They say golf emulates life. I can promise you this: If any of the insanity that is currently taking place in the world right now (2019) were to rear its ugly head on a golf course, I would probably have to develop a new hobby. My golfing days would be over.

CHAPTER 30
Interesting Times

"Do not be anxious about anything, but in everything,
by prayer and petition, with thanksgiving, present your
requests to God. And the peace of God, which transcends
all understanding, will guard your hearts and your
minds in Christ Jesus."

(Philippians 4:6-7)

During a tournament in the Midwest, players on the top-ranked team in the country at the time confronted a couple of my All-Americans about me. They asked if I had been hired at Stanford because of affirmative action. My guys said they scoffed at the notion and mentioned my background. The opposing players took the info and they accepted the alternative narrative. They actually came up to me and initiated a conversation, which later evolved into a solid friendship. I guess the additional vetting satisfied them. We definitely righted the ship within the program. Stanford climbed the polls during my stint in Palo Alto going from No. 42 to No. 1 in the country. Coaching was a perfect fit for me.

After winning the national championship in 2007, I made good on my promise to my wife. She wanted to get back to the East Coast. I left the "Farm" and accepted the top spot at Michigan State University. MSU head football coach Mark Dantonio introduced me during one of his initial press conferences as the new head men's golf coach. The move was easy because it got us closer to North Carolina. A flight back to Greensboro was much easier beginning in Detroit or Lansing, as compared to beginning in San Francisco or San Jose.

The program at MSU was definitely different. The administration was truly on board and really wanted to win, but the focus was on winning conference championships and not national championships.

I was hired by legendary hockey coach Ron Mason, who had become the athletic director. My supervisor was terrific. Senior AD Greg Ianni definitely had my back. When Coach Mason stepped down, MSU hired one of the most creative folks whom I have ever come across in Mark Hollis. I will always be extremely grateful to Coach Mason and Greg Ianni for going against the grain and giving me an opportunity. They allowed me to make history. I became the first African American head coach of a Power Five conference school. (The Power Five includes the major sports conferences: Big Ten, Big 12, Pac-12, Southeast, and Atlantic Coast.)Greg would later tell me that he knew that I would be able to meet local opposition. He had guessed that my upbringing and background had properly prepared me for the challenge. They provided a ton of support and it quickly paid off with the culmination of a Big Ten championship and a Big Ten Coach of the Year Award. The department allowed me to do what I knew how to do, which was recruit and coach. We worked hard and we didn't take any shortcuts. To be fair, I was afraid to take time off or take any shortcuts. I figured being the only black coach at a Power Five conference school would place a target on my back. I was truly afraid to fail because I felt as though I was carrying a lot of other people's hopes and dreams on my shoulders.

The work was intense, but rewarding and exciting. We definitely endured some conference battles.

This wasn't a big deal because I believed then and still do now that the Big Ten is one of the best college golf conferences in the country. After we defeated the University of Illinois in 2008 for the Big Ten championship, Illinois went on an unprecedented run of winning 10 out of the next 11 conference crowns. They have also become a national power and each year play a major role in the national golf landscape.

This episode into coaching in the Midwest also opened up a pandora's box of tolerance. This was truly the first time that I was forced to think twice about who I recruited. This second-guessing was based on their political views and racial tolerance values. The Midwest was a different beast. The liberals in California cared about excellence, changing the world, thinking outside of the box, and all things diversity. The Midwest was made up of a lot of traditional Republican strongholds. Although each state in the Midwest had a large metropolitan city, there was an abundance of rural areas that were centered on farming and agriculture. There was not a lot of diversity in many of these small towns. This was evident during the 2016 presidential election. Donald Trump won Michigan, Minnesota, Indiana, Iowa, Ohio, Nebraska, and Kansas. He also won the states skirting the outside of the Midwest footprint.

I was slightly naive. Although I had travelled through the Midwest while interning for GDT Sports Marketing back in 1991, I had never spent an inordinate amount of time in this part of the country. I met some special people at MSU. There was one thing I dared not forget. Regardless of how much I accomplished and regardless of what I did, I am and will always be only a black man to a lot of people. In their eyes, *black* would definitely precede *coach*. Being the first African American to lead a Power Five conference school was an honor and a privilege, but it didn't come without a lot of haters. I would travel to tournaments with my teams and some competing coaches wouldn't speak. It didn't bother me. It actually motivated me more and kept me focused.

We won tournaments every year at MSU. The team was consistently competitive. We were a perennial top-30 program. A couple of years we finished inside of the top 20 nationally, with eighth being the best. This still didn't prevent folks from calling me a boy and throwing the "N" word at me. Jerks!

I coached All-Americans, all-conference players, all-academic players, future PGA Tour players, and a young man who qualified to play in the Masters. It was an incredible experience, but we must remain obedient because all of our steps are ordered.

My four-year tenure with the MSU Spartans included a Big Ten Coach of the Year Award (2008), a Big Ten Championship title (2008), and a few NCAA appearances. In addition to team accomplishments, my MSU teams registered nine individual tournament wins.

I had been sabotaged by members in the community, yet I was able to win. I actually won a lot. My former supervisor at MSU, Greg Ianni, told me that my reputation in the college world was fantastic. He said that I was called one of the best recruiters in the country and that I always gave our program a chance to win.

I never missed work. I never took a day off. In hindsight this was probably a mistake. I should have moved slower and taken more time to smell the roses. I grinded and the entire department knew it.

There were two episodes that stood out during my coaching career, which reiterated to me that I better keep life in perspective. We had just won the Big Ten championship in 2008 and we were entering a new season with really high expectations. There were two members in the community who literally got life twisted. One of them got upset with me because I refused to place a neighbor's friend's kid on the team. Playing on any athletic team at any university in the country is a privilege and not a birthright. These highly motivated individuals hounded me for months. They called me, emailed me, and literally dropped by my office at their whim. I was always respectful, but I continued to share with them that our roster was full.

During one fateful evening, one of the gentlemen saw my wife leaving the grocery store. He pulled up next to her and forced her to slow down. While driving next to her, he literally cut her off and he made rude and obscene gestures to her while screaming out the window. My children were also in the car. My wife panicked. She grabbed her phone and called 911. The local law enforcement authorities forced the guy and his family to back off with the intimidation tactics. The school supported us through the process.

The second case really got inside my goat. The team had just finished poorly in a tournament out in California. Upon arrival back in the office, I noticed I had several voice messages on my office phone. They were all from the same guy. I am guessing that this guy was about 75 years old. This is only a guess. His message said, "Coach Puryear...we didn't want MSU to hire you and we knew you didn't know what you didn't know. Your people don't know anything about golf and we hope that you go back to where you came from." He then concluded with a few racial phrases that I dare not mention in this book. The comments would hurt my parents knowing that this crap still exists. I was able to brush this to the side and continue to coach. The final incident I experienced was nasty. He was an entitled S.O.B. He also went out of his way to reference me as the terrible "N" word to members of my team. These guys are clowns. I didn't allow words to stop what God had already set in motion.

After four good years and the development of so many wonderful relationships within the athletic department, it had to come to an end. My wife's mom had been diagnosed with dementia and her dad had major kidney failure and he was placed on dialysis. They have since left this earth, but it was only another example that family indeed matters.

Several years later, I connected with Coach Tom Izzo, Coach Dwayne Stephens, and the basketball contingent during the NCAAs in Charlotte. We set it up for MSU to practice at Queens University of Charlotte, and Coach Izzo asked me to say a few words to the team at the conclusion of one of the practices. They were truly salt-of-the-earth folks. I definitely will always cherish those memories.

Due to the family health issues, we left MSU and headed back home. I accepted the position of director of golf at Queens University of Charlotte.

The Queens program was not very good on the women's side and they had enjoyed minimal success on the men's side. I would also be leading the Professional Golf Management Program (PGM). This was exciting because this would increase my influence on young people who were looking to make a career within the golfing industry. My belief was and still is that the game of golf is only as good as the people in it. The job also had another unique caveat. It would be my first time coaching a women's collegiate golf program. I wanted to see if the same methodologies that I utilized on the men's side worked with the women. I knew I would have to speak differently, but I was prepared to work them just as hard. In the history of the university, the women's golf team had never won a conference title. Most of the women enjoyed playing the game, but they viewed it more as a recreational opportunity. I realized in order to be successful, I had to change the mindset, and in order to change the mindset, I had to recruit better, more devoted players.

I watched more than enough junior tournaments in podunk towns up and down the East Coast and all through the South. This was the biggest difference between coaching at a big school and coaching at a small school. The budgets were on opposite ends of the spectrum. I was now forced to drive and watch tournaments with junior players shooting video game scores. I will never forget watching a few junior girls play down in South Carolina. How about this for a foursome: The best score in the group that day was a 98. The other three girls shot 115, 108, and 158 respectively. This was the worse golf that I had ever seen in my life. As I was following different groups, watching them compete, I was wishing that I was one of the Avengers. I wanted a superpower. The special power of invisibility would have served me well during those 6.5 hours. It would have been great to disappear. I had gone to watch three girls play in the event. Two of the three girls were playing behind this group and the third young lady was three holes back. The main young lady I went to see shot a 79 that day. I promised if she came to play for me, she would become the best player in the history of the university. At the conclusion of her fourth year at Queens, she had become the best player in the history of Queens. She had the best stroke average at 72 and she had won more events than any other student-athlete that preceded her. Her final season in college ranked her as one of the top players in Division II. Her name was Grace Glaze, and she truly made my job easy. Welcome to small ball.

Coaching the students at Queens turned out to be a ton of fun. The women's program won back-to-back conference championships in 2011-

12 and 2012-13, which at the time were the only two conference titles in the university's history. I also led the men to a conference title during the 2012-13 season. After qualifying for the NCAA Regionals in the 2013-14 academic year, the team completed the season ranked 23rd in the country. In 2014, I received the honor of South Atlantic Conference Coach of the Year. I also led the Lady Royals to an incredible run in 2016, ending the campaign with another conference title. We won our final four contests of that season, highlighting the most impressive run in the school's history.

My experiment worked and my initial assertions were correct. I found that coaching women was incredible. The women were fantastic to work with and they worked really hard. After six years at Queens, I had amassed three women's conference titles and one men's title along with an additional NCAA appearance.

I learned some valuable lessons as a coach. I learned that pressure bursts pipes. Some of these young people throughout my stops were not built for this pressure. Many of these youth at these major institutions had never had to experience any true adversity. Many of them were completely steamrolled when confronted. This is where the East Lake students excelled. They were born and lived their entire young lives in adversity. They seemed to be tougher and very resilient. These traits were a part of what I searched for as a coach. When I found these traits in recruits, they typically became very good collegiate players and fantastic people.

Conrad Ray, the head coach at Stanford, allowed me to bring Brandon and Shelton out to Palo Alto to work one of our summer golf camps. The guys were incredible. All of the campers were white and they absolutely gravitated toward the boys. Golf was the glue. We can look different, carry different vernaculars, and dress differently, but when you can hit that little white ball and converse like a professional, we are all the same. Becoming a collegiate coach also reaffirmed my initial beliefs that the youth in East Lake had received a first-class introduction to the game of golf, which I also called the game of life. I taught them the game properly and from the inside out. They had to develop a solid short game before spending the crux of their time on the range. My approach and philosophy worked. I learned a lot of lessons from my father, but the culmination of the "village" prepared me for my future.

I also learned a lot from my college coach at Tennessee State University. I played under the leadership of Coach Dr. Catana Starks. This turned out to be legendary. Coach Starks' story was made into a Hollywood movie. She was the first female to coach a men's Division I golf team. I served as a consultant for the movie *From the Rough*, starring Oscar nominees Taraji P. Henson as Coach Starks, Tom Felton of *Harry Potter*, and Michael Clarke Duncan from *The Green Mile*. The movie was surreal. It was amazing for Hollywood to create a story based on the life, sweat, and tears that you experienced.

I am still working with young people, trying to help them foster their dreams. I have now travelled to China, Taiwan, Japan, Dubai, Uganda, Rome, South Africa, and all around the United States in an effort to provide positive opportunities for deserving young people. It has been an incredible journey for me both professionally and personally.

Two of my three children have grown up and graduated from college. Tony has created a successful construction company in Greensboro. I am now a grandfather. My middle child Brooke is currently teaching in Charlotte at a very challenging high school. When she graduated college, she accepted a great job working for Oracle up in Massachusetts. She enjoyed the friends and the pay, but felt a greater calling to come back to Charlotte to work with the underserved.

My baby girl Cameron is currently in college and trying to navigate her way through life.

CHAPTER 31

Teachable Family Lessons

"Therefore encourage one another and build each
other up, just as in fact you are doing."

(1 Thessalonians 5:11)

I will always be grateful for the stories. I am blessed that the residents trusted me. I am appreciative for having had the opportunity to help those who didn't think anyone cared. These folks became an integral part of my life. I think I learned as much from them as they did from me. I developed more compassion and patience. I also think I learned a lot about myself.

I initially spent nine years with a lot of families, but four families in particular inevitably changed my life. This was followed by the past 13 years nurturing and maintaining those relationships. The Davises, the Bradleys, the Lowrys, and the Browns. These relationships molded me into the person I am today. We are not in control. God is in control. I did the best job that I could do with the tools that I had been given. I loved them all. I still love them all, regardless of their path and plight in life. I think God gives us designations with our lives. No one fails in life. We simply have different destinations.

The triumphant escape of several impoverished or socioeconomically disadvantaged children is enough to keep a permanent grin on my face. There is one message in all of this that I would like to trumpet. Trust God and use what He has given us for the good. Help someone and make a positive difference in someone else's life! Do a good turn daily and always be prepared. Many children from the neighborhood didn't make it because a lot of them needed figurative band-aids in their lives to stop the bleeding from their real or imagined life wounds and cuts.

The kids laughed and called themselves Grady babies. This is their affectionate term for being born at Grady Hospital, which is located in downtown Atlanta. When I lived in the ATL, the greater community didn't want anything to do with the hospital. It is funny how time changes everything. Although Grady carried a very negative connotation, the regentrification that consumed the ATL during the early 2000s changed all of the perceptions. Grady is now where the "majority" prefer to go for all of their ailments. These students were the ignition in the neighborhood. If these kids hadn't succeeded in golf, there probably wouldn't be a high school state championship.

The boys were lucky and very fortunate that someone challenged their curriculum and their teachers. They were fortunate that someone was able to make regular announced and unannounced school visits to check on them. They were fortunate that their "dream" light was given new batteries and they were able to reach for the stars.

Everything in life begins with a thought. On my first trip to our after-school program at Greater Piney Baptist Church, which was the site for our initial after-school program, a lot of these students didn't dream about their future. Most of these kids didn't dream about tomorrow. They lived life one day at a time, and they were definitely not armed to look any further. The saddest element in this equation was that their parents were essentially in the same boat. My father always said, "The apple doesn't fall too far from the tree, unless it grows on a hill." These people had been lied to and cheated on so many levels, but the world acknowledges that black folks are the most forgiving people on the planet.

I want this book to serve as an educational blueprint to others. I want kids, parents, or simply concerned citizens, who are either in similar situations or are in situations of influence, to read this and realize that as a community we still have a lot of work to do. Parents should preach and praise effort. Parents should also praise intellect and IQ, but make sure they know the difference. There are communities all around the country that need volunteers. In other words, I want someone to see this and use it to make a difference in someone else's life. All is never lost. We can defy our situations, therefore changing the course of our lives. The plight or educational strength of a parent should not force you or mandate you to place limits on your child's educational journey. If all of us look in the mirror and say aloud that we don't know what we don't know, then it would be easier to allow others to enter and help us.

The book is not meant to insinuate the only path to success is through a traditional collegiate track, and it isn't meant to signify that a college degree guarantees success. Those sentiments are simply not true. The law of averages adamantly opposes these beliefs. What I am proposing is that every child should at least have college on their initial radar screen and in the very least complete high school. Placing college on your radar simply means trying to maximize your opportunities in your math, science, history, economics, and English classes in all levels of schooling. These are the basic principles that simply allow you to live. Balancing a checkbook, developing a great credit score, working toward home ownership, paying bills on time, owning your vehicles, or riding public transportation are all tenants of this basic philosophy. Creating a life full of positive experiences is what makes the world go around.

Statistics in socially challenged communities around the country indicate that many of our youth aren't completing high school. This is public information. This isn't fool's gold. The Atlanta Public School System is a perfect example. Parents and other concerned adults need to recognize that they are privy to all of this information. These statistics can be changed and improved. This is sad. There are no mistakes. The least we should expect from the system is for our children to receive an education. Education is meant to be free. People died for the opportunity to be educated. People were beaten trying to learn to read. Taxpayers should hold their schools and their respective school systems accountable and force them to educate our children.

I can't imagine someone reading this and yet still questioning their family's role in this equation. The family plays a huge role. They are responsible. I was a middle school teacher many years ago, and I can admit that I had children in my classes who didn't want to be there. It bothered me. It truly pissed me off, but it also made me hungrier to teach them. I will admit when I called their home about any situation that the parents would all but curse me out. A lot of these people felt their children could do no wrong.

This is only half of the equation. Discipline and the nurturing of the educational process begins at home. Parents, please take the time with your children when they are young. Look through their weekly folders. Help them read. If you can't read, find someone who can. The government funds a lot of after-school programs. There are probably more programs than you know about that are receiving government funding. The First Tee National School Program, which is there to expose your child to golf, receives millions from the federal government. These programs are there for you. Whether it is a school-run program or junior golf program, there are things that you can do in every community around the country if you are interested in making a difference.

We should be present at local school board meetings, PTA meetings, parent-teacher conferences. We should volunteer at voter precincts and help in your child's classroom. We should be writing letters for our children to our appointed and elected officials. We can make a difference in a unified front. I tear up when I think that Dr. Martin Luther King Jr. and thousands of others were physically and mentally abused in order to provide us voting rights and opportunities. It bugs me because so many of us don't know where the local voting precincts are in our neighborhoods, yet we complain when neighborhood schools close, taxes increase, and job opportunities are reduced.

There are simply no excuses for educational ineptness. The excuses that we didn't attend college, can't get time off from work, or simply work nominal jobs are a major-league cop-out. Parents should understand that education is power. There are people with college degrees who are struggling and many are underemployed, but the degree gives them more options. Factories and certain industries are closing at a record pace. One interesting facet of jobs in America is that the demand for basic jobs is in high demand. The jobs at restaurants, Uber drivers, local post offices, and Walmart are starting to be filled by older, college-degreed personnel. The gap between the haves and have-nots only seems to be increasing.

Parents, please take the time to look online or in the local classified section of the newspapers to check and see what types of jobs are plentiful. If you don't subscribe to either, you can drive or take public transportation to your local library and find the answers to this information. If you don't have the basic skill-set for a job—and trust me, you know if you do or don't—don't get deterred. Visit the local NAACP office, Goodwill, Urban League office, or a bevy of local churches, simply to name a few, to get self-sufficiency classes. These classes include interviewing assistance, resume help, typing instruction, basic math components, and simple life skills.

Please work with your children early and often. Help your child:

- Create a vision for his or her life.

- Discover their innate gifts. (Every child is born with a gift or a special talent.)

- Embrace and encourage their self-worth and teach them life lessons about accountability and responsibility so that failure doesn't become a foreign word, but a part of their evolution. The mark of success is simply bouncing back after some level of disappointment.

- Help them with homework.

- Be the example you wish them to emulate.

- Recognize words are powerful; actions are majestic.

- Place God in their lives.

- Show discipline. Stop trying to be friends with your children. Discipline is love.

CHAPTER 32

Full Circle

"Behold, I will do a new thing; now it shall spring forth;
shall ye not know it? I will even make a way in the
wilderness, [and] rivers in the desert."

(Isaiah 43:19)

I am sitting at the house with family and friends hosting what I think is simply going to be a normal cookout. There are 25 people or more scheduled to come through. I have everything laid out. The food is in abundance and the drinks are plentiful. We are slated to have chicken, steak, fried fish, a bunch of salad, massive amounts of mac and cheese, beans, and burgers. I am actually sitting out back with my dad.

At this point in my life, I value any amount of time I get to spend with my parents. These days, at least for the last 15 years or so, have been very different for my family. My dad lost his sight shortly after having quintuple bypass surgery on his heart. We never noticed any trouble. My dad and I were actually in Atlanta playing golf at East Lake Golf Club. We were walking up the 15th hole, which is set on a really severe incline. As we got to the top of the hill preparing to hit our second shot, I turned and noticed my dad was walking about 20 yards behind me. He seemed to be laboring as he ascended the hill and he was sweating profusely. I

157

shared the situation with my mom and we pressed my dad until he went and got a physical. The appointment revealed a large amount of blockage in all of his arteries. My dad underwent the procedure, but things haven't been the same since. The loss of vision was a little quicker than gradual and it created a drastic change in lifestyle for my mother. She now serves as his eyes.

Although life ransacked my dad's ability to be independent, it only seemed to intensify his faith. His golfing exploits ended when his vision went on a permanent vacation, but his spirits are still fantastic. He is definitely not upset with God. In fact, he has told me on numerous occasions that he is blessed. He believes that he has seen more beautiful things in his times utilizing his eyes than most people will see in a lifetime.

The cookout is in full effect. The Alexa, which is connected to some speakers outside, is blasting music by Drake. Some people are watching the soon-to-be world champion Washington Nationals on the television inside. Folks are everywhere.

The doorbell rings.

My brother comes to the back door and says, "Hey, Sam, someone is at the front door and they want to see you." I kind of try to ignore him since I am chilling with my dad, but he is incredibly persistent. He is giving me that crazy look with the wrinkles in his forehead. His look says, *Man, bring your ass in here and greet whoever is at the door!* I laugh and jump up to see what was happening.

As I walk in the house, I see five large men standing in my kitchen smiling and laughing at me. They all look at me and say, "What up, pops?" Standing in my kitchen are Shelton, Brandon, Rod, Eric, and Willie. These were my East Lake kids. They are now much bigger than me and they are 30 and 31 years old respectively. I haven't been in the presence of all of them at the same time in many, many moons. Gladys, Sheldon, Shelton's fiancée, my brother, and Laura had done me a solid. They met these kids at Brandon's wedding. Brandon got married in Bermuda to a beautiful young lady several months prior and we were blessed to be present to experience it. It was great watching Brandon's mom and dad share an incredibly momentous occasion with their youngest child. I hadn't seen his dad since that fateful day on the driving range 20 years earlier.

I am now in total shock. This is one of the best surprises that I have ever had in my life. These kids are special. They are family, and I have enjoyed watching them grow and evolve into wonderful young men.

Where has the time gone? I have been able to touch a lot of lives and I hope that I am blessed to positively affect thousands more. Success is leased, not owned, and rent is due every day.

These kids made it. They defied the odds and averted becoming senseless statistics. To God be the Glory. I have been blessed.

The story doesn't end here.

On August 22, 2019, NBA All-Star Stephen Curry made the incredible announcement of creating the first Division I golf team for Howard University in Washington, DC. My parents taught me the concept of life being cyclical. The email I recently received proves that theory correct. Howard University offered me the opportunity to become their new Director of Golf. This opportunity allows me to coach and develop both the men's and the women's teams. We will compete at the highest level, excel in the classroom and make a difference in the community. I called my dad to share the good news and his response brought tears. He told me to look up Matthew 3:17. He said the verse came to him and it was exactly how he felt about me. It reads, "And a voice from heaven said, 'This is my Son, whom I love; with him I am well pleased.'"

This is the end of the Diamonds in the Rough story, but only the continuation of leveling the playing field. I am packing up and moving to Washington, DC.

ABOUT THE AUTHOR

Samuel G. Puryear, Jr. was born in Winston-Salem, NC and is an honors graduate of Tennessee State University in Nashville, TN. During Puryear's time as a collegiate golfer and team captain, he played under the leadership of Coach Dr. Catana Starks, the first woman to coach a men's Division I golf team. His coaching career includes Stanford University, Michigan State University, Queens University of Charlotte, and Howard University. He became the first African-American Head Coach at a Power Five Conference university. (MSU 2008)

Puryear's coaching career culminated in 1 national championship, 1 Big Ten Championship, 2 Coach of the Year honors, 2 Conference Carolina Titles and 2 South Atlantic Conference championships. More than 10 of Puryear's former players have played in at least one PGA Tour event.

Puryear is dedicated to maximizing potential in the young people he has worked with and is an advocate for education and professional growth. He found a niche in developing golfers and mentoring new coaches, directing junior golf clinics and camps, adult golf instruction and private corporate outings. Puryear is also a recurring facilitator and coach for Nike's golf camps in the southeast region.

Puryear has been a leader within the golf industry by touching lives and instilling dreams on the collegiate level and within local communities. He started his career in 1998 as the Executive Director of the East lake Junior Golf Academy in Atlanta, Ga. Understanding the importance of junior golf in a community, Puryear was a prominent spokesperson for the topic and directly impacted the revitalization of the East Lake neighborhood, which at one time was saturated with crime. He shared this inspiring story in his new book, *Diamonds in the Rough*.

Currently, Puryear serves as President for Pure Swing Golf Solutions, LLC. With more than 20 years in the golf industry, his specialties include junior golf development for collegiate placement, motivational speaking, mentoring students and coaching. Puryear also worked with junior golfers in China, Taiwan, Dubai, Mexico and Uganda and helped to bring these players to the United States to play golf.

He has extensive experience in developing boards and working with key leaders in sports, banking and finance, entertainment, the legal sector, the nonprofit arena, and faith-based organizations. These relationships have led to the recruitment of top-level volunteers and industry professionals.

Puryear's accolades include being recognized by several media outlets as a prominent spokesperson discussing the future of minorities in golf. He has served on a golf panel on CNN. Puryear's work with student-athletes has also been featured on ESPN and Inside the PGA TOUR. His efforts contributed to a larger community revitalization in metropolitan Atlanta that was prominently featured in *Fortune, The New York Times, USA Today, The Wall Street Journal* and *The Atlanta Journal-Constitution*. Puryear was also featured with two former golf students on the Disney Channel in a segment encouraging kids to follow their dreams.

In 2007, the mayor of Winston-Salem, N.C., Puryear's hometown, proclaimed June 11 "Samuel G. Puryear Jr. Day" because of his contribution to the game of golf and the local community. Most recently, he served as a consultant for making the movie "From the Rough," starring Academy Award nominees Taraji P. Henson as Coach Starks, Tom Felton of "Harry Potter," and Michael Clarke Duncan from "The Green Mile."

Puryear has amassed a bevy of accomplishments, but his biggest joys are his three amazing children and his granddaughter. To learn more, visit https://puryeargolf.com.

CPSIA information can be obtained
at www.ICGtesting.com
Printed in the USA
LVHW021924180121
676816LV00015B/248